Newmark LEARNING

5

Common Core

Reading

Warm-Ups & Test Practice

Newmark Learning
629 Fifth Avenue, Pelham, NY • 10803

Editor: Ellen Ungaro
Designer: Raquel Hernández

Photo credits: Page 34: Courtesy of Library of Congress; Page 43: Sergey Petrov/Shutterstock.com;
Page 54: Courtesy of Dallas Krentzel; Page 93: Courtesy of Yann

Table of Contents

Introduction

What are the new Common Core assessments?

The Common Core State Standards for English Language Arts have set shared, consistent, and clear objectives of what students are expected to learn. The standards are intended to be rigorous and reflect what students will need to be able to do to be college and career ready by the end of high school.

As a part of this initiative, two consortia of states, the Partnership for Assessment of Readiness for College and Careers (PARCC) and Smarter Balanced, have developed new assessments that are aligned with the Common Core State Standards and designed to measure students' progress toward college and career readiness.

How are the new assessments different?

The new standardized assessments from both PARCC and Smarter Balanced are designed to be taken online and include many new types of assessment items.

In addition to multiple-choice questions, the assessments include both short and extended constructed-response questions, which require students to develop written responses that include examples and details from the text.

Another key element in the PARCC and Smarter Balanced assessments is the two-part question. In two-part questions, Part B asks students to identify the text evidence that supports their answer to Part A. These questions reflect the new emphasis on text evidence in the Common Core Standards. Anchor Standard 1 states that students should "cite specific textual evidence when writing or speaking to support conclusions drawn from the text."

The assessments from PARCC and Smarter Balanced also include technology-enhanced questions. These items, which students will encounter if they take the online assessments, ask students to interact with and manipulate text. For example, some questions ask students to select two or three correct answers from a list. Other questions ask students to identify important events in a story and then arrange them in the correct order.

The assessments from PARCC and Smarter Balanced will also feature passages that meet the requirements for complex texts set by the Common Core State Standards. The ability to read and comprehend complex text is another key element of the new standards. Anchor Standard 10 for reading states that students should be able to "Read and comprehend complex literary and informational texts independently and proficiently."

Common Core Reading Warm-Ups & Test Practice is designed to help prepare students for these new assessments from PARCC and Smarter Balanced. The Warm Ups and Practice Tests will help students rehearse the kind of thinking needed for success on the online assessments.

What Test Will Your State Take?

Smarter Balanced States	PARCC States
Alaska	Arizona
California	Arkansas
Connecticut	Colorado
Delaware	District of Columbia
Hawaii	Florida
Idaho	Georgia
Iowa	Illinois
Kansas	Indiana
Maine	Kentucky
Michigan	Louisiana
Missouri	Maryland
Montana	Massachusetts
Nevada	Mississippi
New Hampshire	New Jersey
North Carolina	New Mexico
North Dakota	New York
Oregon	North Dakota
Pennsylvania	Ohio
South Carolina	Oklahoma
South Dakota	Pennsylvania
U.S. Virgin Islands	Rhode Island
Vermont	Tennessee
Washington	
West Virginia	
Wisconsin	
Wyoming	

How will this book help my students prepare for the new assessments?

Warm Ups for Guided Practice

Common Core Reading Warm-Ups & Test Practice includes ten Warm Up tests that are designed to provide students with an opportunity for quick, guided practice.

The ten Warm Ups feature short reading passages that include examples of the genres that students are required to read and will encounter on the test. In grade 5, the Common Core State Standards require students to read stories, drama, poetry, social studies, science, and technical texts.

Fantasy

Poetry

Science Text

Interview

The questions that follow the Warm Ups include the variety of formats and question types that students will encounter on the new assessments. They include two-part questions, constructed response (short answer) questions, and questions that replicate the technology-enhanced items.

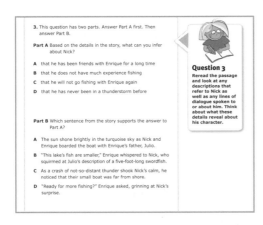

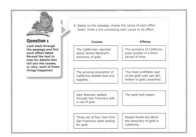

The Warm Ups also include prompts with each question. These prompts provide students with tips and strategies for answering the questions.

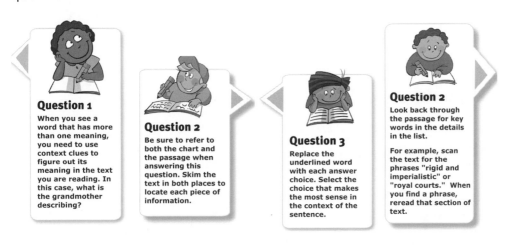

Practice Tests to Build Test-Taking Stamina

The Practice Tests feature longer passages that match the passage lengths that will be used for the PARCC and Smarter Balanced tests. These passages provide students with experience reading the longer and more complex texts they will have to read on the new assessments.

Two of the Practice Tests also feature paired passages. The paired passages give students the opportunity to compare and contrast texts and integrate information from multiple texts, as required by Standard R.9.

Literature

Paired Texts

Informational Text

Each passage is followed by a complete set of questions that reflects the number of questions students will find with each passage on the new assessments. In addition, similar to the Warm Ups, the Practice Tests also include the types of questions students will encounter. Every Practice Test also includes three constructed response (short answer) questions to give students practice writing about texts and using details from the text in their response.

1. This question has two parts. Answer Part A first. Then answer Part B.

Part A What is the main idea of this passage?

A Scientists use satellites to study space because they can fly above the clouds.

B Some satellites use energy from the sun to stay powered while orbiting the Earth.

C The Earth and the moon are examples of natural satellites that orbit larger bodies.

D Satellites are used in many ways to help people communicate with each other and gather information.

Part B Which of the following sentences from the passage support the answer to Part A? Check the box next to each sentence that you choose.

☐ A satellite is a moon, planet, or machine that orbits a planet or star.

☐ For example, Earth is a satellite because it orbits the sun.

☐ If you have a GPS receiver, these satellites can help figure out your exact location.

☐ Some take pictures of the planet that help meteorologists predict weather and track hurricanes.

☐ Satellites come in many shapes and sizes.

☐ The power source can be a solar panel or battery.

☐ Polar-orbiting satellites travel in a north-south direction from pole to pole.

☐ Still other satellites are used mainly for communications, such as beaming TV signals and phone calls around the world.

Two-part Questions

4. Which of the statements below describe a use for satellites from the passage? Check the box next to each statement you choose.

☐ Take pictures of other planets

☐ Track hurricanes

☐ Get rid of dust that blocks the view of the Earth

☐ Beam telephone signals

☐ Send TV signals farther

☐ Change the weather

☐ Help GPS receivers figure out locations

Questions with multiple answers

8. Describe how the author organizes the information in the passage to make it easy for the reader to understand. Use details from the passage to support your answer.

_____

9. Describe the parts of a satellite based on the information in the passage. Use details from the passage to support your answer.

_____

10. Based on the information in the passage, compare and contrast natural and artificial satellites. Use details from the passage to support your answer.

_____

Constructed-response questions

Correlated to the Common Core State Standards

All of the assessment items are correlated to the Reading Standards for Literature or the Reading Standards for Informational Text. The chart below shows the standards that each Warm Up and Practice Test addresses.

TEST	RL/ RL 5.1	RL/ RI 5.2	RL/ RI 5.3	RL/ RI 5.4	RL/ RI 5.5	RL/ RI 5.6	RL/ RI 5.7	RL/ RI 5.8	RL/ RI 5.9
Warm Up 1			X	X		X			
Warm Up 2	X	X						X	
Warm Up 3	X	X	X	X					
Warm Up 4	X	X	X		X				
Warm Up 5			X	X		X			
Warm Up 6			X	X	X				
Warm Up 7	X	X	X						
Warm Up 8		X	X	X		X			
Warm Up 9	X	X	X	X					
Warm Up 10				X		X	X	X	X
Practice Test 1	X	X	X	X	X		X	X	
Practice Test 2	X	X	X	X		X		X	
Practice Test 3	X	X	X	X	X	X			X
Practice Test 4	X	X	X	X	X	X		X	

Grade 5 Common Core State Standards

Reading Standards for Literature

RL.5.1 Quote accurately from a text when explaining what the text says explicitly and when drawing inferences from the text.
RL.5.2 Determine a theme of a story, drama, or poem from details in the text, including how characters in a story or drama respond to challenges or how the speaker in a poem reflects upon a topic; summarize the text.
RL.5.3 Compare and contrast two or more characters, settings, or events in a story or drama, drawing on specific details in the text (e.g., how characters interact).
RL.5.4 Determine the meaning of words and phrases as they are used in a text, including figurative language such as metaphors and similes.
RL.5.5 Explain how a series of chapters, scenes, or stanzas fits together to provide the overall structure of a particular story, drama, or poem.
RL.5.6 Describe how a narrator's or speaker's point of view influences how events are described.
RL.5.7 Analyze how visual and multimedia elements contribute to the meaning, tone, or beauty of a text (e.g., graphic novel, multimedia presentation of fiction, folktale, myth, poem).
RL.5.9 Compare and contrast stories in the same genre (e.g., mysteries and adventure stories) on their approaches to similar themes and topics.

Reading Standards for Informational Texts

RI.5.1 Quote accurately from a text when explaining what the text says explicitly and when drawing inferences from the text.
RI.5.2 Determine two or more main ideas of a text and explain how they are supported by key details; summarize the text.
RI.5.3 Explain the relationships or interactions between two or more individuals, events, ideas, or concepts in a historical, scientific, or technical text based on specific information in the text.
RI.5.4 Determine the meaning of general academic and domain-specific words and phrases in a text relevant to a *grade 5 topic or subject area*.
RI.5.5 Compare and contrast the overall structure (e.g., chronology, comparison, cause/effect, problem/solution) of events, ideas, concepts, or information in two or more texts.
RI.5.6 Analyze multiple accounts of the same event or topic, noting important similarities and differences in the point of view they represent.
RI.5.7 Draw on information from multiple print or digital sources, demonstrating the ability to locate an answer to a question quickly or to solve a problem efficiently.
RI.5.8 Explain how an author uses reasons and evidence to support particular points in a text, identifying which reasons and evidence support which point(s).
RI.5.9 Integrate information from several texts on the same topic in order to write or speak about the subject knowledgeably.

How to Use *Common Core Reading Warm-Ups and Test Practice*

The Warm Ups are designed to be quick and easy practice for students. They can be used in a variety of ways:

- Assign Warm Ups for homework.

- Use them for quick review in class.

- Use them for targeted review of key standards. The correlation chart on page 10 can help identify Warm Ups that address the skills you want to focus on.

The longer Practice Tests can be used to prepare students in the weeks before the assessments. They can also be used to help assess students' reading comprehension throughout the year.

Tear-out Answer Keys

Find the answers to all the Warm Ups and Practice Tests in the Answer Key. The Answer Key includes the standards correlations for each question. In addition, it includes sample answers for the constructed response (short answer) questions.

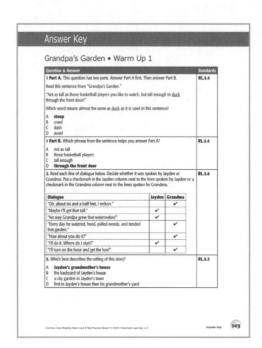

Common Core ELA STANDARDS

RL.5.3
Compare and contrast two or more characters, settings, or events in a story or drama, drawing on specific details in the text (e.g., how characters interact).

RL.5.4
Determine the meaning of words and phrases as they are used in a text, including figurative language such as metaphors and similes.

RL.5.6
Describe how a narrator's or speaker's point of view influences how events are described.

Read this passage and then answer the questions that follow.

Grandpa's Garden

1 Jayden pored over his grandma's old photo albums, struggling to remember his grandfather. There he was, holding Jayden on his lap, a gigantic grin on his face. Everything was gigantic about Grandpa, Jayden recollected—his hands, his feet, his laugh.

2 "Grandma," Jayden questioned, "how tall was Grandpa?"

3 "Oh, about six and a half feet, I reckon. Not as tall as those basketball players you like to watch, but tall enough to duck through the front door!" she chuckled.

4 "Maybe I'll get that tall," Jayden mused.

5 As he turned his attention back to the album, he noticed a series of cryptic photos of fruits and vegetables growing in a garden. There were tomatoes, strawberries, yellow squash, green beans—and, in one snapshot, Jayden's grandpa was hoisting a spotted green watermelon high overhead.

continued ➡

6　　"No way Grandpa grew that watermelon!" exclaimed Jayden.

7　　"Oh, yes, he did," retorted his grandma. "Your granddaddy definitely had a green thumb. He would dig and dig, turning the soil over until it was nice and soft. Then came planting time, and he set all those seeds in the ground by hand. Every day he watered, hoed, pulled weeds, and tended that garden."

8　　"Where was it?" quizzed Jayden.

9　　"Right yonder over there." She motioned with her head to the far side of the backyard.

10　　"I don't see any garden," objected Jayden. "All I see is dirt and grass."

11　　"Yes, well, there is nobody around to tend the garden anymore . . ." his grandma's voice trailed off. "How about you do it?" she said brightly.

12　　"Sounds like a lot of work." Jayden didn't mean to speak that out loud, for he knew his grandmother would be disappointed in his attitude. "All right," he said resolutely. "I'll do it. Where do I start?"

13　　"I'll turn on the hose and get the hoe!" Grandma said, exuberant.

Name_____ Date_____

1. This question has two parts. Answer Part A first. Then answer Part B.

Part A Read this sentence from "Grandpa's Garden."

> "Not as tall as those basketball players you like to watch, but tall enough to <u>duck</u> through the front door!" she chuckled.

Which word means almost the same as <u>duck</u> as it is used in this sentence?

A stoop

B crawl

C dash

D avoid

Part B Which phrase from the sentence helps you answer Part A?

A not as tall

B those basketball players

C tall enough

D through the front door

Question 1

When you see a word that has more than one meaning, you need to use context clues to figure out its meaning in the text you are reading. In this case, what is the grandmother describing?

continued

Name_____ Date_____

Question 2

In a story, the dialogue is the conversation between characters. Look back through the passage. Determine who spoke each line of dialogue, and then check the correct box.

Question 3

Look for clues about the setting throughout the story. Think about what the characters are doing, what they say about the place where the action takes place, and direct descriptions from characters as well as the narrator.

2. Read each line of dialogue below. Decide whether it was spoken by Jayden or Grandma. Put a checkmark in the Jayden column next to the lines spoken by Jayden or a check mark in the Grandma column next to the lines spoken by Grandma.

Dialogue	Jayden	Grandma
"Oh, about six and a half feet, I reckon."	☐	☐
"Maybe I'll get that tall."	☐	☐
"No way Grandpa grew that watermelon!"	☐	☐
"Every day he watered, hoed, pulled weeds, and tended that garden."	☐	☐
"How about you do it?"	☐	☐
"I'll do it. Where do I start?"	☐	☐
"I'll turn on the hose and get the hoe!"	☐	☐

3. Which best describes the setting of this story?

A Jayden's grandmother's house

B the backyard of Jayden's house

C a city garden in Jayden's town

D first in Jayden's house then his grandmother's yard

STOP!

RI.5.1
Quote accurately from a text when explaining what the text says explicitly and when drawing inferences from the text.

RI.5.2
Determine two or more main ideas of a text and explain how they are supported by key details; summarize the text.

RI.5.8
Explain how an author uses reasons and evidence to support particular points in a text, identifying which reasons and evidence support which point(s).

Read this passage and then answer the questions that follow.

Meet Sue

1   On August 12, 1990, a young woman by the name of Susan Hendrickson made a remarkable discovery. Located near the base of a cliff in South Dakota were the fossil remains of a dinosaur. But this was not just any dinosaur. It was a *Tyrannosaurus rex*, the "Tyrant Lizard King." The dinosaur had lain buried for almost 65 million years. As scientists worked to free the fossil from its resting place, they began to understand their amazing find. When fully uncovered, the dinosaur was almost 90 percent complete.

2   In 1997, the dinosaur's bones were put up for auction. In a little over eight minutes, the winning bid was made by the Field Museum of Chicago. The museum offered over $8 million, the largest amount of money ever paid for a fossil. Now the dinosaur had both a home and a purpose.

continued ➡

3 "Sue," named after her discoverer, is considered to be the largest and best-preserved fossil of her kind. She is also the most complete, measuring 42 feet long from snout to tail and standing almost 13 feet tall. Sue weighs an incredible 3,922 pounds; the skull alone weighs 600 pounds. Of the 324 known bones that made up the dinosaur's skeleton, Sue has a total of 224. In fact, Sue's body is so well preserved that scientists are actually able to see where the dinosaur's muscles were located, particularly in the tail area.

4 The *T. rex* was one of the last dinosaur species to live in North America, over 67 million years ago. Because Sue is the most complete dinosaur fossil ever unearthed, she has tremendous value for people who study dinosaurs.

5 Sue continues to be the subject of great fascination among dinosaur lovers all over the world. And with Sue's help, we continue to learn more about these amazing creatures.

Name_____ Date_____

1. This question has two parts. Answer Part A first. Then answer Part B.

Part A What is the main idea of this passage?

A The discovery of a *Tyrannosaurus rex* skeleton in 1990 was a valuable find for scientists.

B The *Tyrannosaurus rex* skeleton found in 1990 was bought for $8 million by a museum in Chicago.

C The *Tyrannosaurus rex* lived in North America more than 67 million years ago.

D The *Tyrannosaurus rex* is the most interesting dinosaur for many reasons.

Question 1
The main idea should be connected to all the information presented in the passage. If you are having trouble coming up with the main idea, think of a short sentence that summarizes the main topic of the text.

Part B Which sentence from the passage helps you answer Part A?

A The dinosaur had lain buried for almost 65 million years.

B The museum offered over $8 million, the largest amount of money ever paid for a fossil.

C Because Sue is the most complete dinosaur fossil ever unearthed, she has tremendous value for people who study dinosaurs.

D Sue continues to be the subject of great fascination among dinosaur lovers all over the world.

continued

Name_____ Date_____

Question 2

Not every detail in a text supports an author's argument. The detail that the museum offered $8 million for the fossil supports the argument that Sue's discovery was remarkable. The text also states that the *T. rex* was the one of the last dinosaur species to live in North America. Does that support the argument that the discovery was remarkable, or is it an interesting detail about dinosaurs?

2. Read this sentence from "Meet Sue."

> On August 12, 1990, a young woman by the name of Susan Hendrickson made a <u>remarkable</u> discovery.

Check the box next to each statement from the passage that supports the author's claim that Susan Hendrickson's discovery was <u>remarkable</u>.

☐ Located near the base of a cliff in South Dakota were the fossil remains of a dinosaur.

☐ When fully uncovered, the dinosaur was almost 90 percent complete.

☐ The museum offered over $8 million, the largest amount of money ever paid for a fossil.

☐ "Sue," named after her discoverer, is considered to be the largest and best-preserved fossil of her kind.

☐ In fact, Sue's body is so well preserved that scientists are actually able to see where the dinosaur's muscles were located, particularly in the tail area.

☐ The *T. rex* was one of the last dinosaur species to live in North America, over 67 million years ago.

☐ And with Sue's help, we continue to learn more about these amazing creatures who once ruled the world.

Name_____ Date_____

3. According to the passage, when did scientists realize the value of the fossil discovered by Susan Hendrickson?

A after it had been studied for years

B when it was sold for $8 million at auction

C when it was being dug up

D when it was moved to a museum in Chicago

Question 3

When a question is asking you to identify the key details, skim the passage for the key words that appear in both the question and the answer choice. Then read the text surrounding the key words to find the answer.

Common **C**ore **ELA** STANDARDS

RL.5.1
Quote accurately from a text when explaining what the text says explicitly and when drawing inferences from the text.

RL.5.2
Determine a theme of a story, drama, or poem from details in the text, including how characters in a story or drama respond to challenges or how the speaker in a poem reflects upon a topic; summarize the text.

RL.5.3
Compare and contrast two or more characters, settings, or events in a story or drama, drawing on specific details in the text (e.g., how characters interact).

RI.5.4
Determine the meaning of words and phrases as they are used in a text, including figurative language such as metaphors and similes.

Read this passage and then answer the questions that follow.

from *The Tangled Threads*

by Eleanor H. Porter

1   To Hester, all the world seemed full of melody. Even the clouds in the sky sailed slowly along in time to a stately march in her brain, or danced to the tune of a merry polka that sounded for her ears alone.

2   Hester was forty now. Two sturdy boys and a girl of nine gave her three hungry mouths to feed and six active feet to keep in holeless stockings. Her husband had been dead two years, and life was a struggle and a problem. The boys she trained, giving just measure of love and care; but the girl—ah, Penelope should have that for which she herself had so longed. Penelope should take music lessons!

3   When the piano finally arrived, Penelope was as enthusiastic as even her mother could wish her to be. It was after the child had left the house, however, that Hester came with reverent step into the darkened room and feasted her eyes to her heart's content on the reality of her dreams. Half fearfully she extended her hand and softly pressed the tip of her fourth finger to one of the ivory keys; then with her thumb she touched another a little below.

4   "Oh, if I only could!" she whispered, and pressed the chord again, rapturously listening to the vibrations as they died away in the quiet room. Then she tiptoed out and closed the door behind her.

continued

Name_____ Date_____

Question 1

When determining the theme, think about an overall message the author is trying to convey through the story. Select the answer choice that best describes that message.

1. This question has two parts. Answer Part A first. Then answer Part B.

Part A Which of these describes a theme in the story?

A Music can be healing.

B Practice makes perfect.

C Childhood is too short.

D Joy can be found in nature.

Part B Which sentence from the passage supports the answer to Part A?

A Her husband had been dead two years, and life was a struggle and a problem.

B Penelope should take music lessons!

C When the piano finally arrived, Penelope was as enthusiastic as even her mother could wish her to be.

D "Oh, if I only could!" she whispered, and pressed the chord again, rapturously listening to the vibrations as they died away in the quiet room.

Name_____ Date_____

2. Why does Hester decide that Penelope should have music lessons and get a piano?

A because Penelope asked to be able to take music lessons

B because Hester loves music and wanted these things as a child

C because Hester's sons are not interested in music

D because Penelope is bored and needs a hobby

Question 2

Reread the passage. Look for the details that describe the moment when Hester decides Penelope should have music lessons.

3. Read this sentence from the passage.

> It was after the child had left the house, however, that Hester came with <u>reverent step</u> into the darkened room and feasted her eyes to her heart's content on the reality of her dreams.

What does the phrase <u>reverent step</u> suggest about Hester's feelings?

A She wants to be quiet at all times.

B She thinks of the piano as a very important possession.

C She is afraid of breaking the piano.

D She wants to keep the piano safe.

Question 3

Authors choose words carefully to show how characters are thinking and feeling. Reread the description of Hester in paragraph 3 and think about what the author is trying to tell the reader about Hester.

STOP!

Read this passage and then answer the questions that follow.

Army Dentist

From kids.usa.gov

1 My name is Captain Ryan Romero and I'm an army dentist.

2 It's our job to make sure that everyone gets an exam every year, and we have to make sure that everybody's dentally fit. If they have any issues dentally, we have to take care of those before they deploy. A deployment is any type of mission where the patient or the service member has to go overseas, and basically stop everything they're doing and help with a mission.

What's your day like?

3 My day typically starts with exam and sick calls. Anything [any person] that walks in the door, from exams to people in severe tooth pain. Some of the things that I like to do are root canals and crowns [putting a cap over the tooth] and bridges [replacing missing teeth].

What is a root canal?

4 A root canal is sometimes needed when somebody has a large cavity that's real close to the nerve and the bacteria have gotten into the nerve and caused pain. So in order to save the tooth, you have to do what's called a root canal.

Common Core ELA STANDARDS

RI.5.1
Quote accurately from a text when explaining what the text says explicitly and when drawing inferences from the text.

RI.5.2
Determine two or more main ideas of a text and explain how they are supported by key details; summarize the text.

RI.5.3
Explain the relationships or interactions between two or more individuals, events, ideas, or concepts in a historical, scientific, or technical text based on specific information in the text.

RI.5.5
Compare and contrast the overall structure (e.g., chronology, comparison, cause/effect, problem/solution) of events, ideas, concepts, or information in two or more texts.

How did you get started?

5   My first job was to be a dental assistant. So I was actually on the other side of the chair helping the dentist. So I enjoyed it so much that I decided to pursue a career in army dentistry.

How to become a dentist

6   I would encourage that they [kids] get really good grades in school. Focus on math and science, for the most part. And another thing I'd suggest is maybe taking an art class. It helps build a foundation for using their hands and that's something that's a very important aspect of dentistry, being comfortable working with your hands.

continued

Name_____ Date_____

Question 1

When determining the main idea, think about all the information in the passage. The main idea is supported by all the details presented by the author.

1. This question has two parts. Answer Part A first. Then answer Part B.

Part A What is the main idea of this passage?

A An army dentist's job is to make sure that people in the army have good dental health.

B An army dentist's day starts with seeing people who are having severe tooth pain.

C In order to become a dentist, you have to get good grades and be good with your hands.

D A root canal is performed when someone has a large cavity that is causing a lot of pain.

Part B Which sentence from the passage supports the answer in Part A?

A My name is Captain Ryan Romero and I'm an army dentist.

B It's our job to make sure that everyone gets an exam every year, and we have to make sure that everybody's dentally fit.

C Anything [any person] that walks in the door, from exams to people in severe tooth pain.

D So in order to save the tooth, you have to do what's called a root canal.

Name_____ Date_____

2. How is the information in this passage organized?

A Each paragraph describes a different part of a dentist's day.

B Each section explains a different problem that a dentist can solve.

C Each section begins with a question and is followed by an answer given by the dentist.

D Different ways to work in dental care are discussed in the paragraphs.

Question 2

Authors have many different ways to organize a text, include describing a sequence of events, comparing and contrasting two things, or explaining the causes and effects. The headings in this text can help you identify the text structure.

3. In what way does the army dentist suggest that taking an art class can be helpful to kids interested in becoming a dentist?

A Taking an art class will help kids become comfortable with their hands.

B Taking an art class will help kids develop a good eye for color.

C Taking an art class will help kids in their math and science classes.

D Taking an art class will help kids get good grades in school.

Question 3

In informational text, the headings can help you locate information because they tell you what each section of the text is about. Think about the information this question is focusing on and scan the headings in this passage. Reread the section where this information is most likely found.

STOP!

RL.5.3
Compare and contrast two or more characters, settings, or events in a story or drama, drawing on specific details in the text (e.g., how characters interact).

RI.5.4
Determine the meaning of words and phrases as they are used in a text, including figurative language such as metaphors and similes.

RL.5.6
Describe how a narrator's or speaker's point of view influences how events are described.

Read this passage and then answer the questions that follow.

One with the Birds

1   It was an amazing day. The sky was a brilliant blue, and the clouds looked like fluffy mounds of cotton. The sea oats waved in the wind as the blue-gray waves crashed against the shore. It was an absolutely perfect dance of nature, thought Joshua.

2   A shrill yell pierced the air: it was Raheem racing across the dunes at breakneck speed. In his hands he was clutching a kite. Joshua sighed. He had promised his mother that he would help Raheem with the kite today. Joshua did not want to be contrary because he adored his mother; but it was criminal to have to spend the day with a baby brother when one could be swimming, fishing, or even just thinking—lying on the sand, watching the ocean. Still, a promise was a promise.

3   Fortunately the day held lots of potential for kite flying. Joshua strolled over to Raheem, who proudly displayed his kite: an oversized piece of cloth and wood, decorated to look like a fierce tiger. Impatient and squirming, Raheem held out the kite. Joshua was continually amazed at how his brother was in constant motion: arms flapping, feet tapping, and, oh yes, mouth moving at the speed of light.

4   Joshua held the kite as Raheem broke into a run, and together the boys raced across the beach, Joshua finally letting the kite loose. Then—airborne! Joshua helped Raheem hold the line. The kite dipped and danced across the sky like a proud peacock, which made Raheem laugh gleefully. The two brothers watched as the seagulls, squawking and cawing, flew around the kite. It was as if the boys had broken some mysterious rule that says that only gulls belong in the sky. But that Sunday, the Clark brothers were one with the birds.

continued

Name_____ Date_____

Question 1

The narrator is the voice of the person telling the story. The narrator is not always a character in the story; sometimes it is a person who can hear the thoughts and know the feelings of one or all of the characters.

1. This question has two parts. Answer Part A first. Then answer Part B.

Part A Which best describes the narrator in this passage?

A an unnamed narrator who describes Joshua's thoughts only

B an unnamed narrator who describes Raheem's thoughts only

C Joshua, who can describe only his own thoughts

D Raheem, who can describe only his own thoughts

Part B How does the narrator of the story show the development of the plot?

A The narrator shows how Raheem feels about spending the day with his brother flying kites by describing his thoughts.

B The narrator shows how the brothers feel about spending the day with each other through their actions.

C The narrator shows how the brothers' feelings about spending the day together change through their words.

D The narrator uses Joshua's thoughts to show how his attitude about spending the day with his brother changes during the story.

Name_____ Date_____

2. Decide whether each detail below describes Joshua or Raheem. Put a checkmark in either the Joshua or Raheem column, depending on which person the detail best describes.

Detail	Joshua	Raheem
promised his mother he would help his brother	☐	☐
full of energy	☐	☐
would rather be alone	☐	☐
did not want to disappoint his mother	☐	☐
has a kite decorated like a tiger	☐	☐
was excited about flying kites	☐	☐
amazed at his brother's energy	☐	☐
laughed gleefully at the flying kite	☐	☐

Question 2
Reread the passage and look for these details as you read. When you find a detail, underline it and write the name of the character it describes above it.

3. Read this sentence from "One with the Birds."

Joshua was <u>continually</u> amazed at how his brother was in constant motion: arms flapping, feet tapping, and, oh yes, mouth moving at the speed of light.

What does the word <u>continually</u> mean?

A hopefully

B repeatedly

C usually

D generally

Question 3
When determining the meaning of an unfamiliar word, looking at the root word can help you figure out the meaning. The root word for *continually* is *continue*.

STOP!

Common Core ELA STANDARDS

RI.5.3
Explain the relationships or interactions between two or more individuals, events, ideas, or concepts in a historical, scientific, or technical text based on specific information in the text.

RI.5.4
Determine the meaning of general academic and domain-specific words and phrases in a text relevant to a *Grade 5 topic or subject area*.

RI.5.5
Compare and contrast the overall structure (e.g., chronology, comparison, cause/ effect, problem/ solution) of events, ideas, concepts, or information in two or more texts.

Read this passage and then answer the questions that follow.

A Discovery as Good as Gold

1   In January of 1848, a sawmill worker in California named James Marshall found a glittering substance in a river. Upon closer inspection, he discovered there were flakes of gold floating down the current. While he was eager to keep his discovery under wraps, it didn't stay secret for long. In March, *The Californian* reported Marshall's lucky find to the public. Although people were wary of the news at first, a fellow named Sam Brannan marched down the streets of San Francisco with a vial of gold dust in his hand. It was the spark that started a fire. The gold rush had commenced.

2   By the summer of 1848, three out of every four men from San Francisco departed from their homes in the hopes of striking it rich. Some panhandlers sifted through dirt in rivers to find flakes of gold much like Marshall and Brannan. Others risked life and limb hacking through deep mountain mines for gold ore, which was larger and much more valuable. People poured in from all over the country and headed west to mine for gold as well. Before the gold rush, there were only around 800 American citizens living in California. By the end of 1849, the population had ballooned to close to 100,000. The need for equipment, as well as food and lodging for the prospectors, helped the California economy boom in a short amount of time.

3   Of course, no enterprise is without risk. The gold rush turned out to be a gamble. Many people bet everything they owned and failed in their bid to find gold. There was something to be said for persistence, however. In 1852, the most profitable year of the gold rush, $81 million in gold was unearthed in the state.

continued ➤

Name_____ Date_____

Question 1

Look back through the passage and find each effect listed. Reread the text to look for details that tell you the causes, or why, each of these things happened.

1. Based on the passage, choose the cause of each effect listed. Draw a line connecting each cause to its effect.

Causes

The Californian reported about James Marshall's discovery of gold.

The growing population of California needed food and supplies.

Sam Brannan walked through San Francisco with a vial of gold.

Three out of four men from San Francisco went looking for gold.

Effects

The economy of California grew quickly in a short period of time.

The most profitable year of the gold rush saw $81 million in gold unearthed.

The gold rush began.

People found out about the discovery of gold in California.

Name_____ Date_____

2. What text structure does the author use to organize most of the information in "A Discovery as Good as Gold"?

A cause and effect

B compare and contrast

C order of importance

D chronological order

3. Read this sentence from "A Discovery as Good as Gold."

> Although people were <u>wary</u> of the news at first, a fellow named Sam Brannan marched down the streets of San Francisco with a vial of gold dust in his hand.

What does the word <u>wary</u> mean?

A cautious

B excited

C uninterested

D eager

Question 2

Signal words can help you determine the text structure. *Because, since,* and *for this reason* signal a cause and effect structure. *Both, like,* and *however* signal a compare and contrast structure. *First, then, before,* and *after,* as well as the use of dates, signal chronological order. *Most importantly* and *secondly* can signal order of importance.

Question 3

When determining the meaning of an unfamiliar word, look for context clues. In this case, the author is making a comparison that can help you understand the word. She is saying that people were cautious at first but became excited after Sam Brannan marched through the streets with his vial of gold dust.

STOP!

Common Core ELA STANDARDS

RL.5.1
Quote accurately from a text when explaining what the text says explicitly and when drawing inferences from the text.

RL.5.2
Determine a theme of a story, drama, or poem from details in the text, including how characters in a story or drama respond to challenges or how the speaker in a poem reflects upon a topic; summarize the text.

RL.5.3
Compare and contrast two or more characters, settings, or events in a story or drama, drawing on specific details in the text (e.g., how characters interact).

Read this passage and then answer the questions that follow.

Courage and Fishing

1   The sun shone brightly in the turquoise sky as Nick and Enrique boarded the boat with Enrique's father, Julio. Nick was a novice at fishing and boating, but he tried to feel courageous as Julio's little vessel cruised the shining lake.

2   "In Puerto Rico," Julio told them, referring to the island where he grew up before coming to Minnesota, "we fished the ocean and caught enormous swordfish and tuna."

3   Enrique taught Nick about bait and hooks in between Julio's stories. "This lake's fish are smaller," Enrique whispered to Nick, who squirmed at Julio's description of a five-foot-long swordfish. "Most are too small, so we'll throw them back; but it's fun anyway."

4   Suddenly, the sky darkened. Over the lake, rain began to fall—first softly, then heavily.

5   Julio frowned. "We must get back to the dock quickly."

6   As a crash of not-so-distant thunder shook Nick's calm, he noticed that their small boat was far from shore. Julio pointed out the dock they would head toward.

7   A nearby cluster of geese spluttered into flight. "They know the water's unsafe during a storm," Enrique said. To reassure Nick, he added, "We'll get ashore."

8   Lightning streaked overhead, and the wind whipped the water into jagged waves that smacked against their boat. Julio called directions about safety to the boys over the shouting thunder.

9   By the time they had reached the dock, secured the boat, and sprinted to a nearby shelter, they were soaked.

10   "The storm will pass; they always do," Julio smiled through hard breaths, perhaps recalling childhood memories. The three of them sat together, watching the sky flash and rage. Within several minutes, the storm cleared, leaving the lake calm again.

11   "Ready for more fishing?" Enrique asked, grinning at Nick's surprise.

12   With a deep breath, Nick gathered his courage and followed his friend to the dock.

continued

Name_____ Date_____

Question 1

When looking for specific details in a story, skim the text and look for key words to help you find the place in the story you need to focus on.

1. Why do Julio, Enrique, and Nick go back to the dock?

A because Nick is scared

B because a storm moves in

C because Julio is done fishing

D because the boys are bored

2. Which sentence represents a theme found in this passage?

A Hard work always pays off.

B Sometimes we have to be brave to get what we want.

C Friendship is more important than anything else.

D Connecting with nature can make your problems seems small.

Question 2

When discussing theme, think about what the characters learn and the ideas that they express in the story. In "Courage and Fishing," what does Nick, the main character, learn?

Name_____ Date_____

3. This question has two parts. Answer Part A first. Then answer Part B.

Part A Based on the details in the story, what can you infer about Nick?

A   that he has been friends with Enrique for a long time

B   that he does not have much experience fishing

C   that he will not go fishing with Enrique again

D   that he has never been in a thunderstorm before

Question 3

Reread the passage and look at any descriptions that refer to Nick as well as any lines of dialogue spoken to or about him. Think about what these details reveal about his character.

Part B Which sentence from the story supports the answer to Part A?

A   The sun shone brightly in the turquoise sky as Nick and Enrique boarded the boat with Enrique's father, Julio.

B   "This lake's fish are smaller," Enrique whispered to Nick, who squirmed at Julio's description of a five-foot-long swordfish.

C   As a crash of not-so-distant thunder shook Nick's calm, he noticed that their small boat was far from shore.

D   "Ready for more fishing?" Enrique asked, grinning at Nick's surprise.

continued

Name_____ Date_____

Question 4

Reread passage and underline any details that show how Nick feels about fishing and underline any details that show how Enrique feels about fishing. Use the details you find to write your answer.

4. Compare how the characters Nick and Enrique each feel about fishing. Use details from the text to support your answer.

_____

_____

_____

_____

_____

_____

_____

Common
Core **ELA**
STANDARDS

RI.5.2
Determine two or
more main ideas of a
text and explain how
they are supported
by key details;
summarize the text.

RI.5.3
Explain the
relationships or
interactions between
two or more
individuals, events,
ideas, or concepts in
a historical, scientific,
or technical text
based on specific
information in the
text.

RI.5.4
Determine the
meaning of general
academic and
domain-specific
words and phrases
in a text relevant to
a *grade 5 topic or
subject area.*

Read this passage and then answer the questions that follow.

Modern Dance

1   Modern dance was born at the start of the twentieth century in the United States. It began when a few choreographers and dancers rebelled against the prevailing forms of dance used at the time. Ballet was seen as rigid and imperialistic, the dance of the royal courts in Europe and Asia. Popular vaudeville shows featured entertainers who danced as part of their funny musical numbers. The desire to find a more fluid expression in dance led to a new style.

2   During the 1920s, a passion for interpretive dancing swept across America. The famous dancer Isadora Duncan, known today as the mother of modern dance, introduced the idea of serious theatrical dancing to the professionals. Its purpose was to showcase emotion through dance and movement in a concert-style performance. The professionals, in turn, passed this on to audiences. This set the stage for the next generation of modern dancers, who further developed the craft.

continued ➤

3   That's not to say that modern dance has not changed since the Great Depression. On the contrary, social and artistic upheavals in the 1960s and 1970s greatly influenced modern dance and helped it evolve. One of the biggest changes in dance was the idea of improvisation. This was a radical departure from the modern dance known forty years earlier.

4   Today's pioneers in the modern dance field have come to embrace ballet. They see ballet as the core foundation of all dancing. As a result, dance companies of all types regard fluency in all dance genres as essential. Today's modern dance is really a fusion of multiple dance genres, including those the original pioneers worked to move away from a century ago.

Name_____ Date_____

1. This question has two parts. Answer Part A first. Then answer Part B.

Part A What is the main idea of this passage?

A Isadora Duncan is known as the mother of modern dance.

B The modern dance movement has evolved since it was born in the first half of the twentieth century.

C Modern dance now incorporates ballet, something dancers rejected when the new genre first began.

D The purpose of modern dance is to showcase emotion through dance.

Question 1

Ignore answer choices that describe a single detail from the text when selecting the correct main idea.

Part B Which sentence from the passage helps you answer Part A?

A Ballet was seen as rigid and imperialistic, the dance of the royal courts in Europe and Asia.

B The famous dancer Isadora Duncan, known today as the mother of modern dance, introduced the idea of serious theatrical dancing to the professionals.

C On the contrary, social and artistic upheavals in the 1960s and 1970s greatly influenced modern dance and helped it evolve.

D They see ballet as the core foundation of all dancing.

continued

Name_____ Date_____

Question 2

Look back through the passage for key words in the details in the list.

For example, scan the text for the phrases "rigid and imperialistic" or "royal courts." When you find a phrase, reread that section of text.

2. Read the following phrases and decide if they describe modern dance or ballet. Put a checkmark in the Modern Dance column if the phrase describes modern dance, or the Ballet column if the phrase describes ballet.

Phrase	Modern Dance	Ballet
rigid and imperialistic	☐	☐
theatrical dancing	☐	☐
seen as the core foundation to dancing	☐	☐
fusion of multiple genres	☐	☐
the dance of European and Asian royal courts	☐	☐
incorporates improvisation	☐	☐

Question 3

Look for the descriptive words to figure out what a vaudeville show would be like. The author talks about "entertainers" and "funny musical numbers."

3. Read this sentence from "Modern Dance."

> Popular vaudeville shows featured entertainers who danced as part of their funny musical numbers.

Based on the information in this sentence, which word would **best** describe a vaudeville show?

A humorous

B mysterious

C serious

D elegant

Name_____ Date_____

4. How did the creators of modern dance view ballet? Compare their point of view to the point of view of modern dancers today. Are they the same or different? Use details from the text to support your answer.

_____

_____

_____

_____

_____

_____

_____

Question 4

To answer this question, start by rereading the text and underlining any details that describe how the creators of modern dance felt about ballet. Then look for any details that describe how today's modern dancers feel about modern dance and underline them. Use these details in your answer.

Read this passage and then answer the questions that follow.

from *The Jungle Book*

by Rudyard Kipling

1   "Something is coming uphill," said Mother Wolf, twitching one ear. "Get ready."

2   The bushes rustled a little in the thicket, and Father Wolf dropped with his haunches under him, ready for his leap. Then, if you had been watching, you would have seen the most wonderful thing in the world—the wolf checked in mid-spring. He made his bound before he saw what it was he was jumping at, and then he tried to stop himself. The result was that he shot up straight into the air for four or five feet, landing almost where he left ground.

3   "Man!" he snapped. "A man's cub. Look!"

4   Directly in front of him, holding on by a low branch, stood a naked brown baby who could just walk—as soft and as dimpled a little atom as ever came to a wolf's cave at night. He looked up into Father Wolf's face, and laughed.

5   "Is that a man's cub?" said Mother Wolf. "I have never seen one. Bring it here."

6   A Wolf accustomed to moving his own cubs can, if necessary, mouth an egg without breaking it, and though Father Wolf's jaws closed right on the child's back not a tooth even scratched the skin as he laid it down among the cubs.

7   "How little! How naked, and—how bold!" said Mother Wolf softly. The baby was pushing his way between the cubs to get close to the warm hide. "Ahai! He is taking his meal with the others. And so this is a man's cub. Now, was there ever a wolf that could boast of a man's cub among her children?"

Common Core ELA STANDARDS

RL.5.1
Quote accurately from a text when explaining what the text says explicitly and when drawing inferences from the text.

RL.5.2
Determine a theme of a story, drama, or poem from details in the text, including how characters in a story or drama respond to challenges or how the speaker in a poem reflects upon a topic; summarize the text.

RL.5.4
Determine the meaning of words and phrases as they are used in a text, including figurative language such as metaphors and similes.

8   "I have heard now and again of such a thing, but never in our Pack or in my time," said Father Wolf. "He is altogether without hair, and I could kill him with a touch of my foot. But see, he looks up and is not afraid."

9   The moonlight was blocked out of the mouth of the cave, for Shere Khan's great square head and shoulders were thrust into the entrance. Tabaqui, behind him, was squeaking: "My lord, my lord, it went in here!"

10   "Shere Khan does us great honor," said Father Wolf, but his eyes were very angry. "What does Shere Khan need?"

11   "My quarry. A man's cub went this way," said Shere Khan. "Its parents have run off. Give it to me."

12   Shere Khan had jumped at a woodcutter's campfire, as Father Wolf had said, and was furious from the pain of his burned feet. But Father Wolf knew that the mouth of the cave was too narrow for a tiger to come in by. Even where he was, Shere Khan's shoulders and forepaws were cramped for want of room, as a man's would be if he tried to fight in a barrel.

13   "The Wolves are a free people," said Father Wolf. "They take orders from the Head of the Pack, and not from any striped cattle-killer. The man's cub is ours—to kill if we choose."

14   "Ye choose and ye do not choose! What talk is this of choosing? By the bull that I killed, am I to stand nosing into your dog's den for my fair dues? It is I, Shere Khan, who speak!"

continued

15   The tiger's roar filled the cave with thunder. Mother Wolf shook herself clear of the cubs and sprang forward, her eyes, like two green moons in the darkness, facing the blazing eyes of Shere Khan.

16   "And it is I, Raksha [The Demon], who answers. The man's cub is mine, Lungri—mine to me! He shall not be killed. He shall live to run with the Pack and to hunt with the Pack; and in the end, look you, hunter of little naked cubs—frog-eater—fish-killer—he shall hunt thee! Now get hence, or by the Sambhur that I killed (I eat no starved cattle), back thou goest to thy mother, burned beast of the jungle, lamer than ever thou camest into the world! Go!"

Name_____ Date_____

1. This question has two parts. Answer Part A first. Then answer Part B.

Part A What can the reader infer based on the details in the story?

A   Shere Khan is more powerful than the wolves.

B   Mother Wolf is afraid of Shere Khan.

C   Father Wolf does not like Shere Khan.

D   Father Wolf is going to kill the baby.

Question 1

Make inferences about characters as you read based on what they say and do, as well as direct descriptions given by the narrator.

Part B Which sentence from the passage helps you answer Part A?

A   The baby was pushing his way between the cubs to get close to the warm hide.

B   He is altogether without hair, and I could kill him with a touch of my foot.

C   The moonlight was blocked out of the mouth of the cave, for Shere Khan's great square head and shoulders were thrust into the entrance.

D   "Shere Khan does us great honor," said Father Wolf, but his eyes were very angry.

continued

Name_____ Date_____

Question 2

When creating a summary, identify the events that are important to the plot of the story. Do not include details or events that are not important to the plot. Cross out any details on this list and then decide the correct order of the summary.

2. Choose the five sentences that belong in a summary of the story and number them in the correct order.

—   The baby laughed.

—   Father Wolf tells Shere Khan that the baby will live with the Wolf family.

—   The mouth of the cave is too narrow for Shere Khan to pass through.

—   Father Wolf takes the baby to his cave.

—   The baby joins the other cubs.

—   Father Wolf finds a baby.

—   Shere Khan asks the wolves for the baby.

—   Mother Wolf has green eyes.

—   Father Wolf was going to pounce until he realized his prey was a baby.

Question 3

Think about the rest of the sentence to determine meaning. In this sentence look at the phrases "want of room" and "fight in a barrel." The sentence before says that the cave was "too narrow." These are all clues to the meaning of the word *cramped*.

3. Read the sentence from *The Jungle Book*.

> Even where he was, Shere Khan's shoulders and forepaws were <u>cramped</u> for want of room, as a man's would be if he tried to fight in a barrel.

What does the word <u>cramped</u> mean in this passage?

A limited

B small

C tucked tightly

D pained

Name_____ Date_____

4. Explain how Father and Mother Wolf feel about Shere Khan. Use details from the passage to support your answer.

_____

_____

_____

_____

_____

_____

_____

Question 4

To answer this question, you will need to make an inference about how Mother and Father Wolf feel by looking at what they say and what they do. For example, look at what Father Wolf says to Shere Khan in paragraph 13. What inference can you make about how Father Wolf feels from this paragraph? Is he afraid of Shere Khan? Does he like her? What other evidence can you find in text to support your answer?

Common Core ELA STANDARDS

RI.5.4
Determine the meaning of general academic and domain-specific words and phrases in a text relevant to *a grade 5 topic or subject area.*

RI.5.6
Describe how a narrator's or speaker's point of view influences how events are described.

RI.5.7
Draw on information from multiple print or digital sources, demonstrating the ability to locate an answer to a question quickly or to solve a problem efficiently.

RI.5.8
Explain how an author uses reasons and evidence to support particular points in a text, identifying which reasons and evidence support which point(s).

Read this passage and then answer the questions that follow.

The Gray Wolf

1   Wolves abound, not only in folklore, but in much of the Northern Hemisphere around the world. They have learned to survive in terrain as varied as mountains, plains, forests, and even deserts.

2   Gray wolves, like all wolves, are part of the canine family. If you were to look at a photograph of a single gray wolf, you might mistake it for a large, long-legged German shepherd.

3   The gray wolf is a particular type of wolf, but don't let its name fool you. While all gray wolves have long, thick fur, not all of them are actually gray. Some are solid white, brown, or even black. There are, however, a few characteristics that they all share. Every gray wolf has a long bushy tail, small triangular ears, long legs, and brown eyes. All wolves also have sharp, pointed teeth, which they use to kill and eat prey.

4   Gray wolves, like all wolves, live in packs, often up to about a dozen members. Each pack has a male and a female leader, known as the *alpha male* and *alpha female*. They are the bosses, and every other wolf in the pack knows it. Should a wolf try to challenge one of the alphas, it would be punished and perhaps banished from the pack. Gray wolves do not like to live alone, so the alphas are rarely challenged.

5   The male and female alphas are mates and remain so throughout their lives. The alphas are the only wolves in the pack to breed. While gray wolves often sleep on the ground out in the open, they establish a den once pups are born. Hollow logs or caves make warm and safe dens. Female gray wolves have also been known to dig dens in the ground for their pups.

6   Both the male and female help raise the pups. The gray wolves are attentive parents and protect their young at all costs. Once a pup reaches the age of about three, it may leave the pack and find a new life, or it may stay with the pack as an adult member.

7   All wolves are carnivores, or meat eaters. Gray wolves hunt deer, elk, beavers, wild rabbits, and even moose. While humans have always been afraid of wolves, humans are not on the list of wolves' natural prey. In fact, most gray wolves seem to fear human beings and will run away as soon as they hear or see a person.

8   Many myths from the past tell of wolf mothers who have found human babies and raised them as their own. Perhaps these stories were told to remind us that while wolves are fierce hunters, they are simply another part of nature, just as we humans are.

continued

Wolves in North America

The gray wolf is not the only type of wolf that lives in North America. Red wolves and eastern wolves are also found in North America.

	Gray Wolf	Red Wolf	Eastern Wolf
Weight	60–120 pounds	45–80 pounds	55–65 pounds
Fur	Gray, black, white, brown	Reddish along the neck and head; mostly brown on their bodies	Reddish brown muzzle and behind the ears and legs; black, white, and gray back
Range	Alaska, Canada, northern United States	Southern Canada, northeastern United States	Canada, New York State
Prey	Elk, beavers, rabbits, moose	Raccoons, rabbits, rodents	Deer, moose, beaver

Name_____ Date_____

1. This question has two parts. Answer Part A first. Then answer Part B.

Part A Which statement **best** describes the information found in the chart?

A   The chart contains facts about wolves in North America.

B   The chart contains information about all types of wolves.

C   The chart contains facts about wolves found around the globe.

D   The chart contains information about how wolves act in their pack.

Part B Which phrase **best** describes why the author included the chart?

A   to show readers what North American wolves look like

B   to help readers find out where to find more information on wolves

C   to help the reader compare and contrast the gray wolf to other North American wolves

D   to show the reader how life in a wolf pack is different for different types of wolves

Question 1

Look at the headings of charts and diagrams to help determine their purpose. In this passage, the title "Wolves in North America" tells the reader what the chart is about. The column headings "Gray Wolf," "Red Wolf," and "Eastern Wolf" give the reader more information about the focus of the chart.

continued ➤

Name_____ Date_____

Question 2

Be sure to refer to both the chart and the passage when answering this question. Skim the text in both places to locate each piece of information.

2. Read each piece of information below. Decide whether the information is found in the passage "The Gray Wolf" or in the chart titled "Wolves in North America." Put a checkmark in the correct box beside each piece of information. If the information is included in both, put checkmarks in both boxes.

Information	The Gray Wolf	Wolves in North America
All wolves live in packs.	☐	☐
All wolves eat only meat.	☐	☐
Gray wolves have long, thick fur.	☐	☐
Red wolves are found in southern Canada and the northeastern United States.	☐	☐
The eastern wolf eats deer, moose, and beaver.	☐	☐
All gray wolves have brown eyes.	☐	☐
Red wolves are smaller than gray and eastern wolves.	☐	☐
The gray wolf can be gray, white, brown, or black.	☐	☐

Name_____ Date_____

3. Read the following sentence from "The Gray Wolf."

> Should a wolf try to challenge one of the alphas, it would be punished and perhaps <u>banished</u> from the pack.

Which does the word <u>banished</u> mean?

A made leader

B raised by other wolves

C forced to fight

D sent away

Question 3

Replace the underlined word with each answer choice. Select the choice that makes the most sense in the context of the sentence.

continued

Name_____ Date_____

Question 4

To identify the author's point of view, reread paragraphs 7 and 8. Does the author think wolves are dangerous to humans? What details does the author include that support that point of view? Underline the details you find and include them in your answer.

4. What is the author's point of view about the relationship between humans and wolves? What evidence does the author use to support his point of view? Give at least two details.

_____

_____

_____

_____

_____

_____

_____

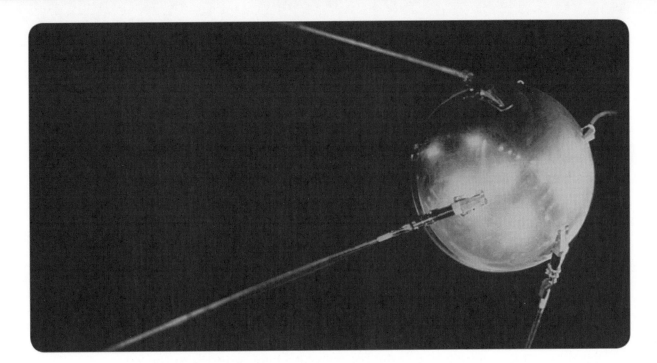

Read the passage. Then answer questions 1–10.

What Is a Satellite?

from www.nasa.gov/audience/forstudents/5-8/features/what-is-a-satellite-58.html

1   A satellite is a moon, planet, or machine that orbits a planet or star. For example, Earth is a satellite because it orbits the sun. Likewise, the moon is a satellite because it orbits Earth. Usually, the word *satellite* refers to a machine that is launched into space and moves around Earth or another body in space.

2   Earth and the moon are examples of natural satellites. Thousands of artificial, or man-made, satellites orbit Earth. Some take pictures of the planet that help meteorologists predict weather and track hurricanes. Some take pictures of other planets, the sun, black holes, dark matter, or faraway galaxies. These pictures help scientists better understand the solar system and universe.

3   Still other satellites are used mainly for communications, such as beaming TV signals and phone calls around the world. A group of more than 20 satellites make up the Global Positioning System, or GPS. If you have a GPS receiver, these satellites can help figure out your exact location.

continued

Why Are Satellites Important?

4　The bird's-eye view that satellites have allows them to see large areas of Earth at one time. This ability means satellites can collect more data, more quickly, than instruments on the ground.

5　Satellites also can see into space better than telescopes on Earth's surface. That's because satellites fly above the clouds, dust, and molecules in the atmosphere that can block the view from ground level.

6　Before satellites, TV signals didn't go very far. TV signals only travel in straight lines. So they would quickly trail off into space instead of following Earth's curve. Sometimes mountains or tall buildings would block them. Phone calls to faraway places were also a problem. Setting up telephone wires over long distances or underwater is difficult and costs a lot of money.

7　With satellites, TV signals and phone calls are sent upward to a satellite. Then, almost instantly, the satellite can send them back down to different locations on Earth.

What Are the Parts of a Satellite?

8　Satellites come in many shapes and sizes. But most have at least two parts in common—an antenna and a power source. The antenna sends and receives information, often to and from Earth. The power source can be a solar panel or battery. Solar panels make power by turning sunlight into electricity.

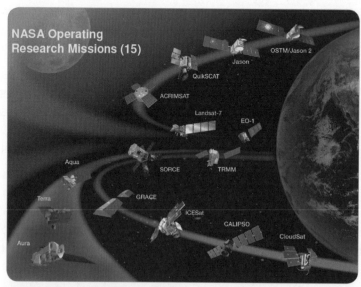

NASA has satellites orbiting Earth to study the land, oceans, and atmosphere.

9   Many NASA satellites carry cameras and scientific sensors. Sometimes these instruments point toward Earth to gather information about its land, air, and water. Other times they face toward space to collect data from the solar system and universe.

How Do Satellites Orbit Earth?

10   Most satellites are launched into space on rockets. A satellite orbits Earth when its speed is balanced by the pull of Earth's gravity. Without this balance, the satellite would fly in a straight line off into space or fall back to Earth. Satellites orbit Earth at different heights, different speeds, and along different paths. The two most common types of orbit are *geostationary* (jee-oh-STAY-shun-air-ee) and *polar*.

11   A geostationary satellite travels from west to east over the equator. It moves in the same direction and at the same rate Earth is spinning. From Earth, a geostationary satellite looks like it is standing still since it is always above the same location.

12   Polar-orbiting satellites travel in a north-south direction from pole to pole. As Earth spins underneath, these satellites can scan the entire globe, one strip at a time.

continued

Name_____ Date_____

1. This question has two parts. Answer Part A first. Then answer Part B.

Part A What is the main idea of this passage?

A   Scientists use satellites to study space because they can fly above the clouds.

B   Some satellites use energy from the sun to stay powered while orbiting the Earth.

C   The Earth and the moon are examples of natural satellites that orbit larger bodies.

D   Satellites are used in many ways to help people communicate with each other and gather information.

Part B Which of the following sentences from the passage support the answer to Part A? Check the box next to each sentence that you choose.

❏   A satellite is a moon, planet, or machine that orbits a planet or star.

❏   For example, Earth is a satellite because it orbits the sun.

❏   If you have a GPS receiver, these satellites can help figure out your exact location.

❏   Some take pictures of the planet that help meteorologists predict weather and track hurricanes.

❏   Satellites come in many shapes and sizes.

❏   The power source can be a solar panel or battery.

❏   Polar-orbiting satellites travel in a north-south direction from pole to pole.

❏   Still other satellites are used mainly for communications, such as beaming TV signals and phone calls around the world.

Name_____ Date_____

2. Based on the information in the passage, how do satellites help meteorologists?

A by sending phone calls

B by beaming TV signals

C by taking pictures of Earth

D by taking pictures of space

3. Read this sentence from the passage.

Most satellites are <u>launched</u> into space on rockets.

Which **best** describes the meaning of <u>launched</u>?

A sent

B orbited

C powered

D watched

4. Which of the statements below describe a use for satellites from the passage? Check the box next to each statement you choose.

☐ Take pictures of other planets

☐ Track hurricanes

☐ Get rid of dust that blocks the view of the Earth

☐ Beam telephone signals

☐ Send TV signals farther

☐ Change the weather

☐ Help GPS receivers figure out locations

continued

Name_____ Date_____

5. The author describes two types of satellites in the passage,
geostationary and polar. Read the list of details below. If the detail
describes a geostationary satellite, check the box in the column labeled
"Geostationary." If the detail describes a polar satellite, check the box
in the column labeled "Polar." Check both boxes if the detail describes
both types of satellites.

Information	Geostationary	Polar
Travels in a north-south direction	❑	❑
Travels over the equator	❑	❑
Is balanced by Earth's gravity	❑	❑
Appears to stand still from Earth	❑	❑
Can scan the entire globe	❑	❑
Moves at the same rate as the Earth spinning	❑	❑
Is launched into space on rockets	❑	❑

6. Read this sentence from the passage.

> The bird's-eye view that satellites have allows them to see
> large areas of Earth at one time.

Why does the author compare the view of a satellite to that of a bird?

A because birds can see at night

B because birds have good eyesight

C because birds see the world from above

D because birds can see over large objects

Name_____ Date_____

7. This question has two parts. Answer Part A first. Then answer Part B.

Part A What inference can you make based on the information in the section "Why Are Satellites Important?"

A Satellites will soon replace all of the telescopes used by scientists.

B Satellites have made it cheaper to send both TV signals and phone calls.

C Satellites are much bigger now than they were when they were invented.

D Satellites have made it easier for people to communicate over long distances.

Part B Which of the following statements support the answer to Part A? Check the box next to each answer you choose.

☐ Satellites can view large areas of Earth at one time and can collect more data, more quickly, than instruments on the ground.

☐ Television signals didn't go very far and were sometimes blocked by mountains and buildings.

☐ Satellites can see into space better than telescopes at Earth's surface.

☐ It is difficult and expensive to set up telephone wires over long distances.

☐ TV signals and phone calls are sent upward to a satellite and then instantly sent back down to different locations on Earth.

☐ Satellites carry cameras and scientific equipment to collect information about the solar system.

continued

Name_____ Date_____

8. Describe how the author organizes the information in the passage
to make it easy for the reader to understand. Use details from the
passage to support your answer.

_____

_____

_____

_____

_____

_____

Name_____ Date_____

9. Describe the parts of a satellite based on the information in the passage. Use details from the passage to support your answer.

_____

_____

_____

_____

_____

_____

_____

Name_____ Date_____

Common Core Reading Warm-Ups & Test Practice Grade 5 • ©2014 Newmark Learning, LLC

10. Based on the information in the passage, compare and contrast natural and artificial satellites. Use details from the passage to support your answer.

_____

_____

_____

_____

_____

_____

_____

_____

_____

_____

_____

_____

_____

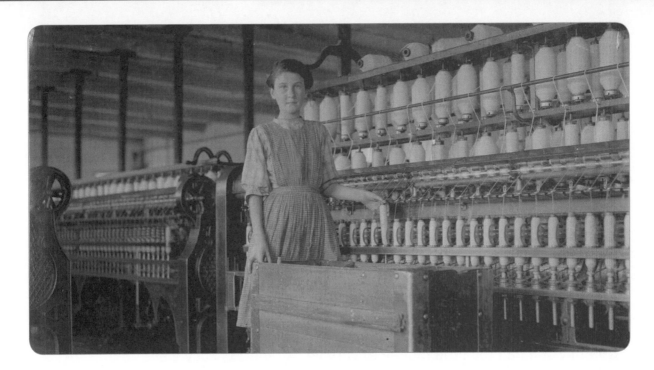

Read the passage. Then answer questions 1–10.

The Mill Girls of Lowell, Massachusetts

1   In the early 1800s, life in America began to change for many people. Most families still lived on farms, but factories were springing up. Inventors were introducing ways to use the energy of falling water to drive machinery. The Industrial Age was beginning.

2   Already, power looms in England were weaving cloth much more quickly than people could weave it at home. Americans were buying this factory-made cloth. An American named Francis Cabot Lowell visited the textile mills in England and took careful note of how the machinery worked. When he returned to America, he hired an engineer to help him create a power loom. He wanted to manufacture cloth in America. In fact, he hoped to create a new community dedicated to textile production.

3   Lowell formed a company called the Boston Associates. In 1814, the Boston Associates built a factory in Waltham, Massachusetts. It was the first mill in the United States that combined all of the operations needed to make finished cloth from raw cotton. Once they had a successful model, Boston Associates bought some land near two rivers. There they built several textile mills powered by water. The brand new industrial city of Lowell was born.

continued ➤

4   But how would the Lowell mills find enough workers? Factory work had a very bad reputation. In England, mill workers lived in desperate poverty. Hoping to build a better kind of community, the mill owners in Lowell decided to recruit young women from farms all over New England. They made the jobs attractive to these new workers. In those days, very few jobs were open to women, and women received extremely low pay. The mill owners offered higher pay. They made sure the young women would have safe, clean places to live, too. They built dormitories and boarding houses near the mills. They set up a strict schedule and rules of behavior for the workers. Bells rang to tell them when to get up, when to start work, when to take their meals, and when to go to bed.

5   Lucy Larcom was one mill worker who wrote about those early days. Lucy's father had died when she was eight. Her mother ran a boarding house in Lowell to support the family. At first, Lucy went to school while helping out at the boarding house, but the family still had too little money to survive. At age 11, Lucy went to work as a "mill girl." Later, she wrote about her experience:

6   *I know that sometimes the confinement of the mill became very wearisome to me. In the sweet June weather I would lean far out of the window, and try not to hear the unceasing clash of sound inside.*

7   Mill work was dirty and noisy. The din of the mechanical looms actually caused some workers to become deaf. For Lucy, it was a daily torment:

8   *I loved quietness. The noise of machinery was particularly distasteful to me. But I discovered that I could so accustom myself to the noise that it became like a silence to me. And I defied the machinery to make me its slave. Its incessant discords could not drown the music of my thoughts if I would let them fly high enough. Even the long hours, the early rising, and the regularity enforced by the clangor of the bell were good discipline for one who was naturally inclined to dally and to dream, and who loved her own personal liberty with a willful rebellion against control.*

9   The mill girls sometimes worked as many as 14 hours a day. Their hours were shorter in the winter. They used their evening hours to get an education and to improve themselves with music and art. They even wrote and published a magazine called *The Lowell Offering*.

10   In 1842, Charles Dickens, a famous writer from England, traveled to America. He went to Lowell to visit the mills. When he returned to England, he published his impressions of America, including some observations he wrote about the Lowell mills:

11   *These girls, as I have said, were all well dressed: and that phrase necessarily includes extreme cleanliness. They had serviceable bonnets, good warm cloaks, and shawls. Moreover, there were places in the mill in which they could deposit these things without injury; and there were conveniences for washing. They were healthy in appearance, many of them remarkably so, and had the manners and deportment of young women: not of degraded brutes of burden.*

12   He went on to say that many of the boarding houses had pianos and that nearly all of the young ladies belonged to circulating libraries. He said that he had read 400 pages of *The Lowell Offering*—a periodical "written exclusively by females actively employed in the mills." These facts, he said, would "startle a large class of readers" in England.

continued

Name_____ Date_____

1. Why did Francis Cabot Lowell visit the textile mills in England?

A to copy their machinery

B to see how mill workers lived

C to write about the mills

D to buy some of their textiles

2. This question has two parts. Answer Part A first. Then answer Part B.

Part A What is the meaning of the word <u>confinement</u> as it is used in paragraph 6?

A constant work

B gossip or chatter

C state of being kept inside

D having little to do

Part B Which phrase from paragraph 6 helps you understand the meaning of <u>confinement</u>?

A know that sometimes

B very wearisome to me

C lean far out of the window

D the unceasing clash of sound

Name_____ Date_____

3. This question has two parts. Answer Part A first. Then answer Part B.

Part A What can you infer about Lucy Larcom from the words she wrote, as quoted in this passage?

A Lucy enjoyed working long hours, getting up early, and sticking to a schedule.

B When Lucy was young, the rigid mill schedule enforced by the bell caused her to feel defiant.

C Lucy came to believe that young people should not be permitted to dally and to dream.

D Lucy was naturally inclined to choose a life of good discipline and regular habits.

Part B Which phrase from Lucy's writing supports the answer to Part A?

A the long hours, the early rising, and the regularity enforced by the clangor of the bell

B good discipline

C one who was naturally inclined to dally

D who loved her own personal liberty with a willful rebellion against control

continued

Name_____ Date_____

4. Read this sentence from the passage.

For Lucy, it was a daily <u>torment</u>.

What is the meaning of the word <u>torment</u>?

A fact of life

B call to action

C symbol of hope

D cause of suffering

5. Both Lucy Larcom and Charles Dickens wrote about the lives of Lowell's mill girls. How are their points of view alike and different? Read each description and decide whether it fits the views of **Lucy Larcom**, **Charles Dickens**, or **Both**. Write a 1 next to answers that fit with Lucy Larcom. Write a 2 next to answers that fit with both. Write a 3 next to answers that fit with Charles Dickens.

—   compared America with England

—   worked in the mills

—   saw good qualities in Lowell mill workers' lives

—   told about negative features of mill work

—   focused on appearances

—   focused on thoughts and feelings

Name_____ Date_____

6. According to the passage, many mill girls found opportunities to improve their lives. Choose three details that provide evidence of opportunities the mill girls found to better themselves.

☐ The workers had bells to tell them when to get up.

☐ Some workers became deaf from loud machinery.

☐ The workers used their evening hours to get an education.

☐ The girls published a magazine called *The Lowell Offering.*

☐ Many girls wore serviceable bonnets.

☐ Most of the workers belonged to circulating libraries.

☐ Many girls began working at when they were eleven years old.

☐ The girls lived in dormitories and boarding houses near the mill.

continued

Name_____ Date_____

7. Choose five sentences that should be included in a summary of this passage and number them in the correct order.

—   In the early 1800s, most American families still lived on farms.

—   The mill girls worked long hours but still found time for education and the arts.

—   Lowell and his associates built America's first successful textile mill.

—   Boston Associates built a new industrial city dedicated to textile production.

—   Francis Cabot Lowell wanted to manufacture cloth in America.

—   The Lowell mill owners recruited young women to work in the mills.

—   The activities of the workday were signaled by the ringing of bells.

—   Charles Dickens described the clothing that the mill girls wore to work.

Name_____ Date_____

8. According to the passage, how was life in America changing for many people in the early 1800s? Describe the major change that was taking place and at least one way it affected people's lives.

_____

_____

_____

_____

_____

_____

9. According to the passage, how did the mill owners make mill jobs attractive to young women? Give at least two details from the passage to support your answer.

_____

_____

_____

_____

_____

_____

_____

continued

Name_____

Name_____ Date_____

Common Core Reading Warm-Ups & Test Practice Grade 5 • ©2014 Newmark Learning, LLC

10. When Charles Dickens said that the facts about mill girls in Lowell would startle many readers in England, what was he suggesting about the mill workers in Lowell and those in England? Use details from the passage to support your response.

_____

_____

_____

_____

_____

_____

_____

_____

_____

_____

_____

_____

_____

Read the passages. Then answer questions 1–10.

Curry without Shortcuts

1   "Mom, we have got to make a dinner dish I just read about. It's called curry, and they say it's sweet, spicy, and savory all at once."

2   Julie had rushed into the living room holding her book open to show her mother the photo. Its caption read, "Curry: Utterly delicious, every time."

3   "Curry—that's adventurous," her mother laughed. "I've never cooked it, but I've tasted it and it's certainly a wondrous flavor."

4   Together they sorted through recipes online, selecting the one that looked easiest. Reading over the list of ingredients, Julie's mother sighed.

5   "We'll have to go to the grocery store; we don't have some of the spices to make this tonight."

6   "But, Mom," Julie objected, "Why don't we just forget about those ingredients and substitute with the things we do have?"

7   Her mother agreed, and they prepared the curry as best they could with the ingredients they had. But when it was time to eat, Julie said, "This doesn't smell or taste nearly as magnificent as my book said it would be."

8   A disappointed look was settling on her mother's face, too. "It isn't anything like the curry I tried at a restaurant once."

continued

9   "I guess we shouldn't have been so impatient. It was silly of me to make us pick the easiest recipe and to leave out important ingredients," Julie said sadly.

10   At school the next day, Julie shared the story of her disappointing curry with her friend Priya.

11   "We can have curry at my house sometime," Priya offered.

12   "Your mom can make curry—real curry, with all of the right spices and recipe steps?" Julie asked, surprised.

13   "My mom can, my dad can, and my sister and I can! We can make it for you and even teach you. It's my grandma's recipe."

14   Priya invited Julie to dinner, and Julie eagerly accepted.

15   Throughout that evening, as Julie cooked with Priya, she became increasingly eager to try genuine curry. Carefully mincing ginger and measuring out coriander and cumin, Priya showed Julie each step and invited her to help. The fragrant aroma of spices whose names Julie hardly recognized surrounded her, and she felt her appetite growing. When dinner was finally ready and they sat down with Priya's family to eat, Julie knew she had never tasted anything similar to this before. For an anxious, fleeting moment, she feared that she might not like it after all: it was strange and new and a bit intimidating. But in a moment of courage, she took a rapid first bite.

16   "What do you think?" Priya asked, giggling at the smile already spreading over Julie's face.

17   Almost embarrassed at her own enthusiasm, Julie said it was just as delightful as she'd imagined.

18   "Now I know that ingredients matter, and sometimes harder recipes are worth the effort," she laughed, recalling her blunder the night before. Indulging in another large bite, she hoped she wouldn't accidentally eat so much that there would be none to share with her mother when she got home!

The Real Princess

by H. C. Andersen

1   There was once a Prince who wished to marry a Princess; but then she must be a real Princess. He traveled all over the world in hopes of finding such a lady; but there was always something wrong. Princesses he found in plenty; but whether they were real Princesses it was impossible for him to decide, for now one thing, now another, seemed to him not quite right about the ladies. At last he returned to his palace quite cast down, because he wished so much to have a real Princess for his wife.

2   One evening a fearful tempest arose, it thundered and lightened, and the rain poured down from the sky in torrents: besides, it was as dark as pitch. All at once there was heard a violent knocking at the door, and the old King, the Prince's father, went out himself to open it.

3   It was a Princess who was standing outside the door. What with the rain and the wind, she was in a sad condition; the water trickled down from her hair, and her clothes clung to her body. She said she was a real Princess.

4   "Ah! We shall soon see that!" thought the old Queen-mother; however, she said not a word of what she was going to do; but went quietly into the bedroom, took all the bed-clothes off the bed, and put three little peas on the bedstead. She then laid twenty mattresses one upon another over the three peas, and put twenty feather beds over the mattresses.

continued

5   Upon this bed the Princess was to pass the night.

6   The next morning she was asked how she had slept. "Oh, very badly indeed!" she replied. "I have scarcely closed my eyes the whole night through. I do not know what was in my bed, but I had something hard under me, and am all over black and blue. It has hurt me so much!"

7   Now it was plain that the lady must be a real Princess, since she had been able to feel the three little peas through the twenty mattresses and twenty feather beds. None but a real Princess could have had such a delicate sense of feeling.

8   The Prince accordingly made her his wife; being now convinced that he had found a real Princess. The three peas were however put into the cabinet of curiosities, where they are still to be seen, provided they are not lost.

Name_____ Date_____

Common Core Reading Warm-Ups & Test Practice Grade 5 • ©2014 Newmark Learning, LLC

1. This question has two parts. Answer Part A first. Then answer Part B.

Part A Read this sentence from "Curry without Shortcuts."

> The <u>fragrant</u> aroma of spices whose names Julie hardly recognized surrounded her, and she felt her appetite growing.

What is the meaning of <u>fragrant</u> as it is used in the sentence above?

A pleasant

B strange

C strong

D unknown

Part B Which phrase from the story helps you understand the meaning of <u>fragrant</u>?

A an anxious, fleeting moment

B she felt her appetite growing

C measuring out coriander and cumin

D she feared that she might not like it

continued

Name_____ Date_____

2. How do the two cooking scenes in "Curry without Shortcuts" fit together to provide the structure to the story?

A They provide a comparison of two characters in the story.

B They provide a contrast that helps show the theme of the story.

C They show two steps leading to the solution of the conflict in the story.

D They tell the cause of a problem and its effect on the characters in the story.

3. Which five sentences should be included in a summary of "Curry without Shortcuts"? Choose the five sentences and number them in the correct order.

___ Julie and her mother decide to make the curry with substituted ingredients.

___ Priya invites Julie over for a curry dinner and shows her how to make a curry dish.

___ Julie's mother doesn't want to go to the grocery store.

___ Julie asks her mother for help making a new recipe for curry.

___ Julie enjoys the curry and realizes the importance of following a recipe.

___ Julie brings the leftover curry home for her mother to enjoy.

___ The curry is a disappointment.

Practice Test 3 • Curry without Shortcuts/The Real Princess

Name_____ Date_____

4. How would "The Real Princess" be different if it were told from the point of view of the Princess? Select the statements that **best** describe how the story would be different. Check the box next to each statement you choose.

☐ The story would include details about how the Princess ended up at the castle.

☐ The story would include more details about what it was like to sleep on the bed.

☐ The story would include the thoughts of all of the characters.

☐ The story would include more details about the castle.

☐ The story would include the thoughts of the Princess.

☐ The story would include more details about the weather.

☐ The story would include details about the different princesses that the Prince met.

☐ The story would include more dialogue between the characters.

continued

Name_____

Name_____ Date_____

5. This question has two parts. Answer Part A first. Then answer Part B.
Read this sentence from "The Real Princess."

> One evening a fearful <u>tempest</u> arose, it thundered and lightened, and the rain poured down from the sky in torrents: besides, it was as dark as pitch.

Part A What is the meaning of <u>tempest</u> as it is used in the sentence above?

A blackout

B flood

C nighttime

D storm

Part B Which detail from the story helps you understand the meaning of <u>tempest</u>?

A One evening

B a violent knocking

C it was as dark as pitch

D it thundered and lightened

Name_____ Date_____

6. What inferences can you make about the Prince based on the story
"The Real Princess"? Check the box next to each statement you choose.

☐   The Prince does not like many people that he meets.

☐   The Prince has spent a long time looking for a Princess to marry.

☐   The Prince is clever and can find ways to tell if a woman is a real
Princess.

☐   The Prince believes that a real Princess has qualities that make her
different from other women.

☐   The Prince is daring and adventurous.

☐   The Prince does not want the Queen-mother's help finding a Princess
to marry.

☐   The Prince would be able to feel the three peas through the twenty
mattresses.

continued

Name_____ Date_____

7. This question has two parts. Answer Part A first. Then answer Part B.

Part A How is the Queen-mother different from the other characters in "The Real Princess"?

A She does not trust other people.

B She takes action to find the truth.

C She thinks she is better than other people.

D She does not want her son to get married.

Part B How is the Queen-mother similar to Priya in "Curry without Shortcuts"?

A They both help solve a problem.

B They both are suspicious of strangers.

C They both spend a lot of time with their families.

D They both are happy when their plan is successful.

Name_____ Date_____

8. What is the theme of "Curry without Shortcuts"? Use details from the passage to support your answer.

_____

_____

_____

_____

_____

_____

9. Summarize the story "The Real Princess."

_____

_____

_____

_____

_____

_____

continued →

Name_____ Date_____

10. How are the problems of Julie in "Curry without Shortcuts" and the
Prince in "The Real Princess" solved? How does each solution reflect
the genre of the story? Use details from both passages to support
your answer.

_____

_____

_____

_____

_____

_____

_____

_____

_____

_____

_____

_____

Read the passages. Then answer questions 1–10.

The Berlin Wall

1   When the people of East and West Berlin went to sleep on the night of August 12, 1961, everything was normal. They expected to wake up the next morning and travel between the two areas to go to work, visit family and friends, and enjoy musical events and soccer games.

2   Instead, they woke up to find that the streets connecting the two sides of the city had been torn up. The East German army had placed concrete posts to block traffic and connected them with barbed wire. Even the telephone lines had been cut.

3   The army had begun building the Berlin Wall. Within a few years, it would stretch more than 100 miles, completely encircling the city of West Berlin. For twenty-eight years, the only way the people of East Berlin could reach West Berlin was by attempting to escape across the wall. Armed soldiers guarded it, ready to shoot any who tried to escape. East Berlin had become a prison.

continued ➤

A Single Country Divided

4   Otto von Bismarck first unified twenty-five independent states under a single German constitution in 1871. Germany functioned as a single country for more than seventy years.

5   Germany was in the center of the two great World Wars in the twentieth century. After being defeated in World War I, Germany had quickly regained its military power. The victors of World War II were determined that this would not happen again. So, in 1945, they sliced Germany in half. The eastern half would be controlled by the communist Soviet Union. The western half would be governed by the United States, France, and Great Britain, known as the Allies.

6   Berlin, the capital and most important city in Germany, was located in the center of the eastern half. The Allies demanded control of the western part of the city, with the Soviet Union controlling the eastern part. West Berlin was like a tiny island surrounded by communist East Germany.

Escaping Communism

7   Within a few years, life in East Germany and West Germany became very different. With the support of the Allies, West Germany soon had a strong economy. Its people worked hard at well-paying jobs. They were able to buy products such as automobiles and refrigerators. They could travel where they wanted and vote in free elections.

8   East Germans were stuck under the communist system forced on them by the Soviet Union. Their economy was weak. The Soviet Union offered little support. People couldn't find jobs or worked for very low pay. They could not speak or travel freely and had no power to choose their own leaders.

9   Many young, talented East Germans wanted to live in West Germany or other free countries. If they could make it to West Berlin, they could fly on to a free country. By 1961, 2.5 million people had fled East Germany. In desperation, the government built a wall to prevent the people from leaving. Still, people risked their lives to escape. About 5,000 people succeeded, although hundreds of others were captured or killed. East Germany, supported by the Soviet Union, continually strengthened the wall to prevent escapes. Eventually, the concrete was about twelve feet high and four feet thick. A smooth pipe at the top prevented people from climbing over it.

A Dramatic Ending

10   By 1989, Communism was failing across Europe. When some neighboring countries overthrew Communism, East Germans gained new ways to escape. The East German government faced increasing opposition.

11   On the evening of November 9, 1989, a German official mistakenly announced that people could pass through the wall whenever they wanted. Thousands of people went to the checkpoints that night and demanded to be let through. The guards were unprepared and eventually opened the gates. Within hours, a huge celebration began on both sides of the wall. People sang and cried in joy. They chipped pieces from the concrete wall with hammers and saved the pieces as reminders of the hard times they had endured.

12   Germany soon became a united country once again. The Berlin Wall has been removed. Signs and exhibits mark the location, reminding visitors of the time when Berlin and the rest of Germany were divided. This place reminds us that many people risked their lives for freedom.

continued

Tear Down This Wall!

1   In 1981, Ronald Reagan became the fortieth president of the United States. Many believe that one of Reagan's major accomplishments was helping reunite a divided Germany. This was a result of historic peace talks between Reagan and Mikhail Gorbachev, the leader of the Soviet Union.

2   Reagan had a long history of speaking out against the Soviet Union and Communism. He did so during his two terms as governor of California, as well as during his presidency. However, in his second term as president, Reagan began to believe that improved communication was possible. For many years, there were strained relations between the United States and the Soviet Union. Reagan was instrumental in bringing the two countries together. Reagan and Gorbachev signed a peace treaty during a period of new openness and freedom in Russia known as *glasnost*. The Intermediate-Range Nuclear-Force Missile Treaty (INF Treaty) played a large role in ending the Cold War. With this treaty, intermediate nuclear forces were reduced.

3   During the talks, Gorbachev visited the United States and Reagan traveled to the Soviet Union four times between 1985 and 1988. On one memorable trip in 1987, Reagan visited the famous Berlin Wall in Germany. The wall had been built to separate East and West Berlin. It blocked people from East Germany who were trying to migrate west. In his speech at the wall, Reagan made an emotional plea to Gorbachev.

4   *General Secretary Gorbachev, if you seek peace, if you seek prosperity for the Soviet Union and Eastern Europe, if you seek liberalization: Come here to this gate! Mr. Gorbachev, open this gate! Mr. Gorbachev, tear down this wall!*

5   This section of Reagan's speech was controversial because people were afraid that they were words that could encourage war. Violence did not occur, but his plea did strike a chord with people in the Soviet Union. There was already a movement growing toward freedom, and Reagan's speech propelled it forward. Many see it as a turning point in the Cold War.

6   Although it took two-and-a-half years, finally, in 1989, after the end of Reagan's presidency, East Germany opened the Berlin Wall to citizens and travelers. In September of 1990, Reagan visited the site of the Berlin Wall to swing a hammer at a broken piece of wall as a symbol of tearing down barriers and opening the gates to freedom.

1. This question has two parts. Answer Part A first. Then answer Part B.

Part A What is the meaning of the word <u>unified</u> as it is used in paragraph 4 of "The Berlin Wall"?

A conquered

B ruled

C made into one

D freed from prison

Part B Which phrase from paragraph 4 supports the answer to Part A?

A independent states

B German constitution

C functioned as a single country

D more than seventy years

2. Which three statements from the passage "The Berlin Wall" support the idea that the Soviet Union wanted to stop people from leaving East Germany? Place a check in the box next to each statement you choose.

☐ Germany functioned as a single country for more than seventy years.

☐ For twenty-eight years, the only way the people of East Germany could reach West Berlin was by attempting to escape across the wall.

☐ Germany was in the center of the two great World Wars in the twentieth century.

☐ About 5,000 people succeeded, although hundreds of others were captured or killed.

☐ By 1961, East Germany had lost 2.5 million people.

☐ In desperation, the government built a wall to prevent the people from leaving.

☐ Instead, they woke up to find that the streets connecting the two sides of the city had been torn up.

continued →

Name_____ Date_____

3. How does the author of "The Berlin Wall" support the point that there were many reasons why people in East Germany wanted to move to West Germany?

A By describing details of daily life in East and West Germany.

B By contrasting the jobs and freedoms in East and West Germany.

C By comparing life before and after East and West Germany were separated.

D By stating where people could go once they left East Germany for West Germany.

4. This question has two parts. Answer Part A first. Then answer Part B.

Part A According to "The Berlin Wall," why did the victors of World War II divide Germany in half?

A They wanted Germany to be separated like Berlin.

B They wanted part of Germany to be just like the Soviet Union.

C They wanted to stop Germany from becoming powerful again.

D They wanted to return Germany to the way it was before World War I.

Part B Which detail from the passage supports the answer to Part A?

A Germany functioned as a single country for more than seventy years.

B After being defeated in World War I, Germany had quickly regained its military power.

C Berlin, the capital and most important city in Germany, was located in the center of the eastern half.

D East Germans were stuck under the communist system forced on them by the Soviet Union.

Name_____ Date_____

5. This question has two parts. Answer Part A first. Then answer Part B.

Part A Read this sentence from "Tear Down This Wall!"

> This was a result of <u>historic</u> peace talks between Reagan and Mikhail Gorbachev, the leader of the Soviet Union.

What does the word <u>historic</u> mean as it is used in this sentence?

A important

B not expected

C happening in the past

D never taking place before

Part B According to the passage, why were the peace talks <u>historic</u>?

A They happened many years ago.

B They helped bring about great change in the world.

C They took place between the United States and the Soviet Union.

D They continued the work Reagan had begun as governor of California.

6. Choose the five sentences that would be included in a summary of "Tear Down This Wall!" Number the sentences in the correct order.

____ East Germany opened the Berlin Wall.

____ The Berlin Wall had been built at the end of World War II.

____ Reagan and Gorbachev held talks and signed a peace treaty.

____ Reagan's speech caused more people in the Soviet Union to want freedom.

____ Reagan had long been against Communism.

____ During a trip to Berlin, Reagan asked Gorbachev to tear down the Berlin Wall.

____ Reagan's achievements made him a great president.

continued

Name_____ Date_____

7. What is the overall structure of "The Berlin Wall" and "Tear Down This Wall!"?

A cause/effect

B chronological

C comparison

D problem/solution

8. Explain the reasons that East Germans wanted to escape to West Germany. Use details from the passage "The Berlin Wall" to support your response.

_____

_____

_____

_____

_____

_____

_____

Name_____ Date_____

9. What inference can be made about the author's opinion of Ronald Reagan in "Tear Down This Wall!"? Use details from the passage to support your answer.

_____

_____

_____

_____

_____

_____

_____

continued

Name_____ Date_____

10. How are "The Berlin Wall" and "Tear Down This Wall!" different in their explanations of why the Berlin Wall was taken down? How do these explanations reflect the different points of view of the passages? Use details from both passages to support your answer.

_____

_____

_____

_____

_____

_____

_____

_____

_____

_____

_____

_____

Grandpa's Garden • Warm Up 1

Question & Answer	Standards
1 Part A. This question has two parts. Answer Part A first. Then answer Part B. Read this sentence from "Grandpa's Garden." "Not as tall as those basketball players you like to watch, but tall enough to <u>duck</u> through the front door!" Which word means almost the same as <u>duck</u> as it is used in this sentence? A **stoop** B crawl C dash D avoid	RL.5.4
1 Part B. Which phrase from the sentence helps you answer Part A? A not as tall B those basketball players C tall enough D **through the front door**	RL.5.4
2. Read each line of dialogue below. Decide whether it was spoken by Jayden or Grandma. Put a checkmark in the Jayden column next to the lines spoken by Jayden or a checkmark in the Grandma column next to the lines spoken by Grandma.	RL.5.6
3. Which best describes the setting of this story? A **Jayden's grandmother's house** B the backyard of Jayden's house C a city garden in Jayden's town D first in Jayden's house then his grandmother's yard	RL.5.3

Dialogue	Jayden	Grandma
"Oh, about six and a half feet, I reckon."		✔
"Maybe I'll get that tall."	✔	
"No way Grandpa grew that watermelon!"	✔	
"Every day he watered, hoed, pulled weeds, and tended that garden."		✔
"How about you do it?"		✔
"I'll do it. Where do I start?"	✔	
"I'll turn on the hose and get the hoe!"		✔

Meet Sue • Warm Up 2

Question & Answer	Standards
1 Part A. What is the main idea of this passage? A **The discovery of a _Tyrannosaurus rex_ skeleton in 1990 was a valuable find for scientists.** B The _Tyrannosaurus rex_ skeleton found in 1990 was bought for $8 million by a museum in Chicago. C The _Tyrannosaurus rex_ lived in North America more than 67 million years ago. D The _Tyrannosaurus rex_ is the most interesting dinosaur for many reasons.	**RI.5.2**
2 Part B. Which sentence from the passage helps you answer Part A? A The dinosaur had lain buried for almost 65 million years. B The museum offered over $8 million, the largest amount of money ever paid for a fossil. C **Because Sue is the most complete dinosaur fossil ever unearthed, she has tremendous value for people who study dinosaurs.** D Sue continues to be the subject of great fascination among dinosaur lovers all over the world.	**RI.5.1**
2. Check the box next to each statement from the passage that supports the author's claim that Susan Hendrickson's discovery was <u>remarkable</u>. Located near the base of a cliff in South Dakota were the fossil remains of a dinosaur. **When fully uncovered, the dinosaur was almost 90 percent complete.** **The museum offered over $8 million, the largest amount of money ever paid for a fossil.** **"Sue," named after her discoverer, is considered to be the largest and best-preserved fossil of her kind.** **In fact, Sue's body is so well preserved that scientists are actually able to see where the dinosaur's muscles were located, particularly in the tail area.** The _T. rex_ was one of the last dinosaur species to live in North America, over 67 million years ago. And with Sue's help, we continue to learn more about these amazing creatures who once ruled the world.	**RI.5.8**
3. According to the passage, when did scientists realize the value of the fossil discovered by Susan Hendrickson? A after it had been studied for years B when it was sold for $8 million at auction C **when it was being dug up** D when it was moved to a museum in Chicago	**RI.5.2**

From *The Tangled Threads* • Warm Up 3

Question & Answer	Standards
1 Part A. This question has two parts. Answer Part A first. Then answer Part B. Which of these describes a theme in the story? A **Music can be healing.** B Practice makes perfect. C Childhood is too short. D Joy can be found in nature.	**RL.5.2**
1 Part B. Which sentence from the passage supports the answer to Part A? A Her husband had been dead two years, and life was a struggle and a problem. B Penelope should take music lessons! C When the piano finally arrived, Penelope was as enthusiastic as even her mother could wish her to be. D **"Oh, if I only could!" she whispered, and pressed the chord again, rapturously listening to the vibrations as they died away in the quiet room**	**RL.5.1**
2. Why does Hester decide that Penelope should have music lessons and get a piano? A because Penelope asked to be able to take music lessons B **because Hester loves music and wanted these things as a child** C because Hester's sons are not interested in music D because Penelope is bored and needs a hobby	**RL.5.3**
3. Read this sentence from the passage. It was after the child had left the house, however, that Hester came with <u>reverent step</u> into the darkened room and feasted her eyes to her heart's content on the reality of her dreams. What does the phrase <u>reverent step</u> suggest about Hester's feelings? A She wants to be quiet at all times. B **She thinks of the piano as a very important possession.** C She is afraid of breaking the piano. D She wants to keep the piano safe.	**RL.5.4**

Army Dentist • Warm Up 4

Question & Answer	Standards
1 Part A. This question has two parts. Answer Part A first. Then answer Part B. What is the main idea of this passage? A **An army dentist's job is to make sure that people in the army have good dental health.** B An army dentist's day starts with seeing people who are having severe tooth pain. C In order to become a dentist, you have to get good grades and be good with your hands. D A root canal is performed when someone has a large cavity that is causing a lot of pain.	RI.5.2
1 Part B. Which sentence from the passage supports the answer in Part A? A My name is Captain Ryan Romero and I'm an army dentist. B **It's our job to make sure that everyone gets an exam every year, and we have to make sure that everybody's dentally fit.** C Anything [any person] that walks in the door, from exams to people in severe tooth pain. D So in order to save the tooth, you have to do what's called a root canal.	RI.5.1
2. How is the information in this passage organized? A Each paragraph describes a different part of a dentist's day. B Each section explains a different problem that a dentist can solve. C **Each section begins with a question and is followed by an answer given by the dentist.** D Different ways to work in dental care are discussed in the paragraphs.	RI.5.5
3. In what way does the army dentist suggest that taking an art class can be helpful to kids interested in becoming a dentist? A **Taking an art class will help kids become comfortable with their hands.** B Taking an art class will help kids develop a good eye for color. C Taking an art class will help kids in their math and science classes. D Taking an art class will help kids get good grades in school.	RI.5.3

One with the Birds • Warm Up 5

Question & Answer	Standards
1 Part A. This question has two parts. Answer Part A first. Then answer Part B. Which best describes the narrator in this passage? A **an unnamed narrator who describes Joshua's thoughts only** B an unnamed narrator who describes Raheem's thoughts only C Joshua, who can describe only his own thoughts D Raheem, who can describe only his own thoughts	RL.5.6
1 Part B. How does the narrator of the story show the development of the plot? A The narrator shows how Raheem feels about spending the day with his brother flying kites by describing his thoughts. B The narrator shows how the brothers feel about spending the day with each other through their actions. C The narrator shows how the brothers' feelings about spending the day together change through their words. D **The narrator uses Joshua's thoughts to show how his attitude about spending the day with his brother changes during the story.**	RL.5.6
2. Decide whether each detail below describes Joshua or Raheem. Put a checkmark in the correct box beside each piece of information. If the information is included in both passages, put checkmarks in both boxes.	RL.5.3

Detail	Joshua	Raheem
promised his mother he would help his brother	✔	
full of energy		✔
would rather be alone	✔	
did not want to disappoint his mother	✔	
has a kite decorated like a tiger		✔
was excited about flying kites		✔
amazed at his brother's energy	✔	
laughed gleefully at the flying kite		✔

Question & Answer	Standards
3. Read this sentence from "One with the Birds." Joshua was <u>continually</u> amazed at how his brother was in constant motion: arms flapping, feet tapping, and, oh yes, mouth moving at the speed of light. What does the word <u>continually</u> mean? A hopefully B **repeatedly** C usually D generally	RL.5.4

A Discovery as Good as Gold • Warm Up 6

Question & Answer	Standards
1. Based on the passage, choose the cause of each effect listed. Draw a line connecting each cause to its effect.	**RI.5.3**

Causes	Effects
The *Californian* reported about James Marshall's discovery of gold.	The economy of California grew quickly in a short period of time.
The growing population of California needed food and supplies.	The most profitable year of the gold rush saw $81 million in gold unearthed.
Sam Brannan walked through San Francisco with a vial of gold.	The gold rush began.
Three out of four men from San Francisco went looking for gold.	People found out about the discovery of gold in California.

Question & Answer	Standards
2. What text structure does the author use to organize most of the information in "A Discovery as Good as Gold"? A cause and effect B compare and contrast C order of importance D **chronological order**	**RI.5.5**
3. Read this sentence from "A Discovery as Good as Gold." Although people were <u>wary</u> of the news at first, a fellow named Sam Brannan marched down the streets of San Francisco with a vial of gold dust in his hand. What does the word <u>wary</u> mean? A **cautious** B excited C uninterested D eager	**RI.5.4**

Courage and Fishing • Warm Up 7

Question & Answer	Standards
1. Why do Julio, Enrique, and Nick go back to the dock? A because Nick is scared B **because a storm moves in** C because Julio is done fishing D because the boys are bored	**RL.5.2**
2. Which sentence represents a theme found in this passage? A Hard work always pays off. B **Sometimes we have to be brave to get what we want.** C Friendship is more important than anything else. D Connecting with nature can make your problems seems small.	**RL.5.2**
3 Part A. This question has two parts. Answer Part A first. Then answer Part B. Based on the details in the story, what can you infer about Nick? A that he has been friends with Enrique for a long time B **that he does not have much experience fishing** C that he will not go fishing with Enrique again D that he has never been in a thunderstorm before	**RL.5.1**
3 Part B. Which sentence from the story supports the answer to Part A? A The sun shone brightly in the turquoise sky as Nick and Enrique boarded the boat with Enrique's father, Julio. B **"This lake's fish are smaller," Enrique whispered to Nick, who squirmed at Julio's description of a five-foot-long swordfish.** C As a crash of not-so-distant thunder shook Nick's calm, he noticed that their small boat was far from shore. D "Ready for more fishing?" Enrique asked, grinning at Nick's surprise.	**RL.5.1**
4. Compare how the characters Enrique and Nick each feel about fishing. Use details from the text to support your answer. **Sample answer:** Nick is nervous about fishing. The text says that he is "trying to be courageous." It also says that he "squirmed" when Julio described the swordfish. Enrique is an experienced and excited about fishing. He teaches Nick about baits and hooks and he thinks fishing is fun even if they have to throw back most of the fish.	**RL.5.3**

Question & Answer	Standards
1 Part A. This question has two parts. Answer Part A first. Then answer Part B. What is the main idea of this passage? A Isadora Duncan is known as the mother of modern dance. B **The modern dance movement has evolved since it was born in the first half of the twentieth century.** C Modern dance now incorporates ballet, something dancers rejected when the new genre first began. D The purpose of modern dance is to showcase emotion through dance.	RI.5.2
1 Part B. Which sentence from the passage helps you answer Part A? A Ballet was seen as rigid and imperialistic, the dance of the royal courts in Europe and Asia. B The famous dancer Isadora Duncan, known today as the mother of modern dance, introduced the idea of serious theatrical dancing to the professionals. C **On the contrary, social and artistic upheavals in the 1960s and 1970s greatly influenced modern dance and helped it evolve.** D They see ballet as the core foundation of all dancing.	RI.5.2
2. Read the following phrases and decide if they describe modern dance or ballet. Put a checkmark in the Modern Dance column if the phrase describes modern dance, or the Ballet column if the phrase describes ballet.	RI.5.3

Phrase	Modern Dance	Ballet
rigid and imperialistic		✔
theatrical dancing	✔	
seen as the core foundation to dancing		✔
fusion of multiple genres	✔	
the dance of European and Asian royal courts		✔
incorporates improvisation	✔	

Question & Answer	Standards
3. Read this sentence from "Modern Dance." Popular vaudeville shows featured entertainers who danced as part of their funny musical numbers. Based on the information in this sentence, which word would best describe a vaudeville show? A **humorous** B mysterious C serious D elegant	RI.5.4

Modern Dance • Warm Up 8

Question & Answer	Standards
4. How did the creators of modern dance view ballet? Compare their point of view to the point of view of modern dancers today. Are they the same or different? Use details from the text to support your answer. **Sample answer:** The creators of modern dance and today's modern dancers have different points of view about ballet. The creators of modern dance felt ballet was too rigid and wanted "to rebel" against it. Today's modern dancers believe that ballet is the foundation of all dance.	**RI.5.6**

From *The Jungle Book* • Warm Up 9

Question & Answer	Standards
1 Part A. This question has two parts. Answer Part A first. Then answer Part B. What can the reader infer based on the details in the story? A Shere Khan is more powerful than the wolves. B Mother Wolf is afraid of Shere Khan. C **Father Wolf does not like Shere Khan.** D Father Wolf is going to kill the baby.	**RL.5.2**
1 Part B. Which sentence from the passage helps you answer Part A? A The baby was pushing his way between the cubs to get close to the warm hide. B He is altogether without hair, and I could kill him with a touch of my foot. C The moonlight was blocked out of the mouth of the cave, for Shere Khan's great square head and shoulders were thrust into the entrance. D **"Shere Khan does us great honor," said Father Wolf, but his eyes were very angry.**	**RL.5.1**

2. Choose the five sentences that belong in a summary of the story and number them in the correct order.
 	
    The baby laughed.
4   Father Wolf tells Shere Khan that the baby will live with the Wolf family.
    The mouth of the cave is too narrow for Shere Khan to pass through.
3   Father Wolf takes the baby to his cave.
5   The baby joins the other cubs.
1   Father Wolf finds a baby.
    Shere Khan asks the wolves for the baby.
    Mother Wolf has green eyes.
2   Father Wolf was going to pounce until he realized his prey was a baby.
	RL.5.2

3. Read the sentence from *The Jungle Book*. Even where he was, Shere Khan's shoulders and forepaws were <u>cramped</u> for want of room, as a man's would be if he tried to fight in a barrel. What does the word <u>cramped</u> mean in this passage? A limited B small C **tucked tightly** D pained	**RL.5.4**

   ©2014 Newmark Learning, LLC

Question & Answer	Standards
4. Explain how Father and Mother Wolf feel about Shere Khan. Use details from the passage to support your answer. **Sample answer:** Father and Mother Wolf are wary of Shere Khan, and Father Wolf is angry that Shere Khan intrudes into their den. But they will not back down from him. Father and Mother Wolf do not respect Shere Khan as a hunter because he only hunts the small, sick, and weak. Mother Wolf calls him a "frog-eater," and Father Wolf calls him a "cattle-killer."	**RL.5.3**

The Gray Wolf • Warm Up 10

Question & Answer	Standards
1 Part A. Which statement best describes the information found in the chart? A **The chart contains facts about wolves in North America.** B The chart contains information about all types of wolves. C The chart contains facts about wolves found around the globe. D The chart contains information about how wolves act in their pack.	**RI.5.7**
1 Part B. Which phrase best describes why the author included the chart? A to show readers what North American wolves look like B to help readers find out where to find more information on wolves C **to help the reader compare and contrast the gray wolf to other North American wolves** D to show the reader how life in a wolf pack is different for different types of wolves	**RI.5.8**
2. Read each piece of information below. Decide whether the information is found in the passage "The Gray Wolf" or in the chart titled "Wolves in North America." Put a check-mark in the correct box beside each piece of information. If the information is included in both, put checkmarks in both boxes.	**RI.5.7**

Information	The Gray Wolf	Wolves in North America
All wolves live in packs.	✔	
All wolves eat only meat.	✔	✔
Gray wolves have long, thick fur.	✔	
Red wolves are found in southern Canada and the northeastern United States.		✔
The eastern wolf eats deer, moose, and beaver.		✔
All gray wolves have brown eyes.	✔	
Red wolves are smaller than gray and eastern wolves.		✔
The gray wolf can be gray, white, brown, or black.	✔	✔

Question & Answer	Standards
3. Which does the word <u>banished</u> mean? A made leader B raised by other wolves C forced to fight D **sent away**	**RI.5.4**

Question & Answer	Standards
4. What is the author's point of view about the relationship between humans and wolves? What evidence does the author use to support his or her point of view? Give at least two details. **Sample answer:** The author's point of view is that wolves are not dangerous to humans. The evidence that the author provides includes the fact that humans are not prey for wolves and that wolves run away from humans instead of attacking them.	**RI.5.6**

What Is a Satellite? • Practice Test 1

Question & Answer	Standards
1 Part A. What is the main idea of this passage? A Scientists use satellites to study space because they can fly above the clouds. B Some satellites use energy from the sun to stay powered while orbiting the Earth. C The Earth and the moon are examples of natural satellites that orbit larger bodies. **D Satellites are used in many ways to help people communicate with each other and gather information.**	**RI.5.2**
1 Part B. Which of the following sentences from the passage support the answer to Part A? Check the box next to each sentence that you choose. ❑ A satellite is a moon, planet, or machine that orbits a planet or star. ❑ For example, Earth is a satellite because it orbits the sun. ❑ **If you have a GPS receiver, these satellites can help figure out your exact location.** ❑ **Some take pictures of the planet that help meteorologists predict weather and track hurricanes.** ❑ Satellites come in many shapes and sizes. ❑ The power source can be a solar panel or battery. ❑ Polar-orbiting satellites travel in a north-south direction from pole to pole. ❑ **Still other satellites are used mainly for communications, such as beaming TV signals and phone calls around the world.**	**RI.5.1**
2. Based on the information in the passage, how do satellites help meteorologists? A by sending phone calls B by beaming TV signals **C by taking pictures of Earth** D by taking pictures of space	**RI.5.3**
3. Read this sentence from the passage. Most satellites are launched into space on rockets. Which best describes the meaning of launched? **A sent** B orbited C powered D watched	**RI.5.4**
4. Which of the statements below describe a use for satellites from the passage? Check the box next to each statement you choose. ❑ **Take pictures of other planets** ❑ **Track hurricanes** ❑ Get rid of dust that blocks the view of the Earth ❑ **Beam telephone signals** ❑ **Send TV signals farther** ❑ Change the weather ❑ **Help GPS receivers figure out locations**	**RI.5.3**

Question & Answer	Standards
5. Read the list of details below. If the detail describes a geostationary satellite, check the box in the column labeled "Geostationary." If the detail describes a polar satellite, check the box in the column labeled "Polar." Check both boxes if the detail describes both types of satellites.	**RI.5.3**

Information	Geostationary	Polar
Travels in a north-south direction		✔
Travels over the equator	✔	
Is balanced by Earth's gravity	✔	✔
Appears to stand still from Earth	✔	
Can scan the entire globe		✔
Moves at the same rate as the Earth spinning	✔	
Is launched into space on rockets	✔	✔

Question & Answer	Standards
6. Read this sentence from the passage. The <u>bird's-eye view</u> that satellites have allows them to see large areas of Earth at one time. Why does the author compare the view of a satellite to that of a bird? A because birds can see at night B because birds have good eyesight C **because birds see the world from above** D because birds can see over large objects	**RI.5.4**
7 Part A. This question has two parts. Answer Part A first. Then answer Part B. What inference can you make based on the information in the section "Why Are Satellites Important?" A Satellites will soon replace all of the telescopes used by scientists. B Satellites have made it cheaper to send both TV signals and phone calls. C Satellites are much bigger now than they were when they were invented. D **Satellites have made it easier for people to communicate over long distances.**	**RI.5.1**
7 Part B. Which of the following statements support the answer to Part A? Check the box next to each answer you choose. ❏ Satellites can view large areas of Earth at one time and can collect more data, more quickly, than instruments on the ground. ❏ **Television signals didn't go very far and were sometimes blocked by mountains and buildings.** ❏ Satellites can see into space better than telescopes at Earth's surface. ❏ **It is difficult and expensive to set up telephone wires over long distances.** ❏ **TV signals and phone calls are sent upward to a satellite and then instantly sent back down to different locations on Earth.** ❏ Satellites carry cameras and scientific equipment to collect information about the solar system.	**RI.5.1, RI.5.8**

Question & Answer	Standards
8. Describe how the author organizes the information in the passage to make it easy for the reader to understand. Use details from the passage to support your answer. **Sample answer:** The author organizes the information in this passage into sections. Each section has a title that lets the reader know what kind of information will be discussed. Each section has a main idea and supporting details that support the main idea of the passage.	**RI.5.5**
9. Describe the parts of a satellite based on the information in the passage. Use details from the passage to support your answer. **Sample answer:** Each satellite has a power source and an antenna. Satellites can carry cameras and scientific sensors. These can be used to gather information about the Earth or space.	**RI.5.1, RI.5.3**
10. Based on the information in the passage, compare and contrast natural and artificial satellites. Use details from the passage to support your answer. **Sample answer:** Both types of satellites orbit larger bodies. Both the moon and Earth are natural satellites. The moon orbits Earth and Earth orbits the sun. Artificial satellites are man-made and they are launched into space by rockets. Man-made satellites are used to gather information about Earth or space or to help people communicate.	**RI.5.1, RI.5.3**

The Mill Girls of Lowell, Massachusetts • Practice Test 2

Question & Answer	Standards
1. Why did Francis Cabot Lowell visit the textile mills in England? A **to copy their machinery** B to see how mill workers lived C to write about the mills D to buy some of their textiles	**RI.5.3**
2 Part A. This question has two parts. Answer Part A first. Then answer Part B. What is the meaning of the word <u>confinement</u> as it is used in paragraph 6? A constant work B gossip or chatter C **state of being kept inside** D having little to do	**RI.5.4**
2 Part B. Which phrase from paragraph 6 helps you understand the meaning of <u>confinement</u>? A know that sometimes B very wearisome to me C **lean far out of the window** D the unceasing clash of sound	**RI.5.1**
3 Part A. This question has two parts. Answer Part A first. Then answer Part B. What can you infer about Lucy Larcom from the words she wrote, as quoted in this passage? A Lucy enjoyed working long hours, getting up early, and sticking to a schedule. B **When Lucy was young, the rigid mill schedule enforced by the bell caused her to feel defiant.** C Lucy came to believe that young people should not be permitted to dally and to dream. D Lucy was naturally inclined to choose a life of good discipline and regular habits.	**RI.5.8**
3 Part B. Which phrase from Lucy's writing supports the answer to Part A? A the long hours, the early rising, and the regularity enforced by the clangor of the bell B good discipline C one who was naturally inclined to dally D **who loved her own personal liberty with a willful rebellion against control**	**RI.5.1**
4. Read this sentence from the passage. For Lucy, it was a daily torment. What is the meaning of the word torment? A fact of life B call to action C symbol of hope D **cause of suffering**	**RI.5.4**

Question & Answer	Standards
5. Both Lucy Larcom and Charles Dickens wrote about the lives of Lowell's mill girls. How are their points of view alike and different? Read each description and decide whether it fits the views of **Lucy Larcom, Charles Dickens,** or **Both.** Write a 1 next to answers that fit with Lucy Larcom. Write a 2 next to answers that fit with both. Write a 3 next to answers that fit with Charles Dickens. compared America with England **[3]** worked in the mills **[1]** saw good qualities in Lowell mill workers' lives **[2]** told about negative features of mill work **[1]** focused on appearances **[3]** focused on thoughts and feelings **[1]**	**RI.5.6**
6. According to the passage, many mill girls found opportunities to improve their lives. Choose three details that provide evidence of opportunities the mill girls found to better themselves. ❑ The workers had bells to tell them when to get up. ❑ Some workers became deaf from loud machinery. ❑ **The workers used their evening hours to get an education.** ❑ **The girls published a magazine called *The Lowell Offering*.** ❑ Many girls wore serviceable bonnets. ❑ **Most of the workers belonged to circulating libraries.** ❑ Many girls began working at when they were eleven years old. ❑ The girls lived in dormitories and boarding houses near the mill.	**RI.5.8**
7. Choose five sentences that should be included in a summary of this passage and number them in the correct order. In the early 1800s, most American families still lived on farms. The mill girls worked long hours but still found time for education and the arts. **[5]** Lowell and his associates built America's first successful textile mill. **[2]** Boston Associates built a new industrial city dedicated to textile production. **[3]** Francis Cabot Lowell wanted to manufacture cloth in America. **[1]** The Lowell mill owners recruited young women to work in the mills. **[4]** The activities of the workday were signaled by the ringing of bells. Charles Dickens described the clothing that the mill girls wore to work.	**RI.5.2**
8. According to the passage, how was life in America changing for many people in the early 1800s? Describe the major change that was taking place and at least one way it affected people's lives. **Sample answer:** The major change that was taking place in the early 1800s was the beginning of the Industrial Age. Many people left farming to work in factories. And, for the first time, many young girls got job opportunities.	**RI.5.2**
9. According to the passage, how did the mill owners make mill jobs attractive to young women? Give at least two details from the passage to support your answer. **Sample answer:** The mill owners offered women higher pay than they could earn in other jobs that were open to them. The owners also provided safe, clean places for the young women to live.	**RI.5.8**

Question & Answer	Standards
10. When Charles Dickens said that the facts about mill girls in Lowell would startle many readers in England, what was he suggesting about the mill workers in Lowell and those in England? Use details from the passage to support your response. **Sample answer:** Charles Dickens suggested that the mill girls in Lowell had advantages that those in England did not have. He explained that the Lowell mill girls were well dressed and clean and "healthy in appearance." He also said that the mills provided places for the girls to deposit their bonnets, cloaks, and shawls "without injury," as well as "conveniences for washing." He would probably not mention any of these facts if they were also true for mill workers in England at the time. In addition, the workers in Lowell had access to pianos and libraries. They wrote and published a periodical called *The Lowell Offering*. These facts help the reader infer that Dickens thought the Lowell mill girls had far better lives than English mill workers.	RI.5.8

Curry without Shortcuts • The Real Princess • Practice Test 3

Question & Answer	Standards
1 Part A. This question has two parts. Answer Part A first. Then answer Part B. Read this sentence from "Curry without Shortcuts." The <u>fragrant</u> aroma of spices whose names Julie hardly recognized surrounded her, and she felt her appetite growing. What is the meaning of <u>fragrant</u> as it is used in the sentence above? A **pleasant** B strange C strong D unknown	RL.5.4
1 Part B. Which phrase from the story helps you understand the meaning of fragrant? A an anxious, fleeting moment B **she felt her appetite growing** C measuring out coriander and cumin D she feared that she might not like it	RL.5.4
2. How do the two cooking scenes in "Curry without Shortcuts" fit together to provide the structure to the story? A They provide a comparison of two characters in the story. B **They provide a contrast that helps show the theme of the story.** C They show two steps leading to the solution of the conflict in the story. D They tell the cause of a problem and its effect on the characters in the story.	RL.5.5
3. Which five sentences should be included in a summary of "Curry without Shortcuts"? Choose the five sentences and number them in the correct order. Julie and her mother decide to make the curry with substituted ingredients. **[2]** Priya invites Julie over for a curry dinner and shows her how to make a curry dish. **[4]** Julie's mother doesn't want to go to the grocery store. Julie asks her mother for help making a new recipe for curry. **[1]** Julie enjoys the curry and realizes the importance of following a recipe. **[5]** Julie brings the leftover curry home for her mother to enjoy. The curry is a disappointment. **[3]**	RL.5.2

Question & Answer	Standards
4. How would "The Real Princess" be different if it were told from the point of view of the Princess? Select the statements that best describe how the story would be different. Check the box next to each statement you choose. ❏ **The story would include details about how the Princess ended up at the castle.** ❏ The story would include more details about what it was like to sleep on the bed. ❏ The story would include the thoughts of all of the characters. ❏ The story would include more details about the castle. ❏ **The story would include the thoughts of the Princess.** ❏ The story would include more details about the weather. ❏ The story would include details about the different princesses that the Prince met. ❏ The story would include more dialogue between the characters.	**RL.5.6**
5 Part A. This question has two parts. Answer Part A first. Then answer Part B. Read this sentence from "The Real Princess." One evening a fearful <u>tempest</u> arose, it thundered and lightened, and the rain poured down from the sky in torrents: besides, it was as dark as pitch. What is the meaning of <u>tempest</u> as it is used in the sentence above? A blackout B flood C nighttime D **storm**	**RL.5.4**
5 Part B. Which detail from the story helps you understand the meaning of <u>tempest</u>? A One evening B a violent knocking C it was as dark as pitch D **it thundered and lightened**	**RL.5.4**
6. What inferences can you make about the Prince based on the story "The Real Princess"? Check the box next to each statement you choose. ❏ The Prince does not like many people that he meets. ❏ **The Prince has spent a long time looking for a Princess to marry.** ❏ The Prince is clever and can find ways to tell if a woman is a real Princess. ❏ **The Prince believes that a real Princess has qualities that make her different from other women.** ❏ The Prince is daring and adventurous. ❏ The Prince does not want the Queen-mother's help finding a Princess to marry. ❏ The Prince would be able to feel the three peas through the twenty mattresses.	**RL.5.1**

Question & Answer	Standards
7 Part A. This question has two parts. Answer Part A first. Then answer Part B. How is the Queen-mother different from the other characters in "The Real Princess"? A She does not trust other people. B **She takes action to find the truth.** C She thinks she is better than other people. D She does not want her son to get married.	**RL.5.3**
7 Part B. How is the Queen-mother similar to Priya in "Curry without Shortcuts"? A **They both help solve a problem.** B They both are suspicious of strangers. C They both spend a lot of time with their families. D They both are happy when their plan is successful.	**RL.5.3**
8. What is the theme of "Curry without Shortcuts"? Use details from the passage to support your answer. **Sample answer:** The theme of "Curry without Shortcuts" is that a person should take the time to do something right. When Julie and her mother rush into making the curry without the correct ingredients, they are "disappointed" with the results. However, when Julie takes the time and makes the effort to prepare the curry the right way, "[c]arefully mincing ginger and measuring out" the other spices, she is rewarded with a "delightful" meal. Julie realizes at the end of the story that "harder" things "are worth the effort."	**RL.5.1, RL.5.2**
9. Summarize the story "The Real Princess." **Sample answer:** There once was a prince who long searched, without success, for a real princess to marry. One night during a storm, a girl who claimed to be a real princess appeared at his castle. In order to test her claim, the Queen-mother placed three peas under a pile of forty beds and mattress for the girl to sleep on. In the morning, the girl complained that she could not sleep because of the hard, painful objects in her bed. This proved that the girl was a real princess, and the prince married her.	**RL.5.2**

Question & Answer	Standards
10. How are the problems of Julie in "Curry without Shortcuts" and the Prince in "The Real Princess" solved? How does each solution reflect the genre of the story? Use details from both passages to support your answer. **Sample answer:** The problems of both Julie in "Curry without Shortcuts" and the Prince in "The Real Princess" are solved with the help of other characters. In "Curry without Shortcuts," Priya helps solve Julie's problem by offering to teach Julie how to make a real curry the correct way. When they are cooking, Priya "showed Julie each step and invited her to help." This solution makes sense for a realistic fiction story in which problems are often solved by friends helping each other and working together to find a realistic solution. In "The Real Princess," the Prince's problem is solved with the help of his mother. Unlike Priya, the Queen does not work with her son but secretly sets up the beds with the hidden peas to find out if the girl is a real princess. This solution makes sense for a fairy tale. Unrealistic, magical events often occur as solutions to problems in fairy tales.	**RL.5.1, RL.5.9**

The Berlin Wall • Tear Down This Wall! • Practice Test 4

Question & Answer	Standards
1 Part A. This question has two parts. Answer Part A first. Then answer Part B. What is the meaning of the word <u>unified</u> as it is used in paragraph 4 of "The Berlin Wall"? A conquered B ruled C **made into one** D freed from prison	**RI.5.4**
1 Part B. Which phrase from paragraph 4 supports the answer to Part A? A independent states B German constitution C **functioned as a single country** D more than seventy years	**RI.5.4**
2. Which three statements from the passage "The Berlin Wall" support the idea that the Soviet Union wanted to stop people from leaving East Germany? Place a check in the box next to each statement you choose. ❏ Germany functioned as a single country for more than seventy years. ❏ For twenty-eight years, the only way the people of East Germany could reach West Berlin was by attempting to escape across the wall. ❏ Germany was in the center of the two great World Wars in the twentieth century. ❏ **About 5,000 people succeeded, although hundreds of others were captured or killed.** ❏ By 1961, East Germany had lost 2.5 million people. ❏ **In desperation, the government built a wall to prevent the people from leaving.** ❏ Instead, they woke up to find that the streets connecting the two sides of the city had been torn up.	**RI.5.2**
3. How does the author of "The Berlin Wall" support the point that there were many reasons why people in East Germany wanted to move to West Germany? A By describing details of daily life in East and West Germany. B **By contrasting the jobs and freedoms in East and West Germany.** C By comparing life before and after East and West Germany were separated. D By stating where people could go once they left East Germany for West Germany.	**RI.5.8**
4 Part A. This question has two parts. Answer Part A first. Then answer Part B. According to "The Berlin Wall," why did the victors of World War II divide Germany in half? A They wanted Germany to be separated like Berlin. B They wanted part of Germany to be just like the Soviet Union. C They wanted to stop Germany from becoming powerful again. D **They wanted to return Germany to the way it was before World War I.**	**RI.5.3**

Question & Answer	Standards
4 Part B. Which detail from the passage supports the answer to Part A? A Germany functioned as a single country for more than seventy years. B **After being defeated in World War I, Germany had quickly regained its military power.** C Berlin, the capital and most important city in Germany, was located in the center of the eastern half. D East Germans were stuck under the communist system forced on them by the Soviet Union.	**RI.5.1**
5 Part A. This question has two parts. Answer Part A first. Then answer Part B. Read this sentence from "Tear Down This Wall!" This was a result of <u>historic</u> peace talks between Reagan and Mikhail Gorbachev, the leader of the Soviet Union. What does the word <u>historic</u> mean as it is used in this sentence? A **important** B not expected C happening in the past D never taking place before	**RI.5.4**
5 Part B. According to the passage, why were the peace talks <u>historic</u>? A They happened many years ago. B **They helped bring about great change in the world.** C They took place between the United States and the Soviet Union. D They continued the work Reagan had begun as governor of California.	**RI.5.1**
6. Choose the five sentences that would be included in a summary of "Tear Down This Wall!" Number the sentences in the correct order. East Germany opened the Berlin Wall. **[5]** The Berlin Wall had been built at the end of World War II. Reagan and Gorbachev held talks and signed a peace treaty. **[2]** Reagan's speech caused more people in the Soviet Union to want freedom. **[4]** Reagan had long been against Communism. **[1]** During a trip to Berlin, Reagan asked Gorbachev to tear down the Berlin Wall. **[3]** Reagan's achievements made him a great president.	**RI.5.2**
7. What is the overall structure of "The Berlin Wall" and "Tear Down This Wall!"? A cause/effect B **chronological** C comparison D problem/solution	**RI.5.5**

Question & Answer	Standards
8. Explain the reasons that East Germans wanted to escape to West Germany. Use details from the passage "The Berlin Wall" to support your response. **Sample answer:** East Germans wanted to escape because they wanted freedom and economic opportunity. The economy in East Germany was not good. There were few jobs and pay was low. People couldn't travel where they wanted or communicate freely. They could not choose their own leaders.	**RI.5.2**
9. What inference can be made about the author's opinion of Ronald Reagan in "Tear Down This Wall!"? Use details from the passage to support your answer. **Sample answer:** The author of "Tear Down This Wall!" admires Ronald Reagan and feels he did a good and important job during his presidency. The author says Reagan "was instrumental in bringing" the United States and the Soviet Union together and creating a better, more peaceful relationship between the two countries. The author also focuses on all of the work that Reagan did to help free the people of East Germany. Reagan's speech to Gorbachev at the Berlin Wall helped improve the lives of many people by "opening the gates of freedom."	**RI.5.1**
10. How are "The Berlin Wall" and "Tear Down This Wall!" different in their explanations of why the Berlin Wall was taken down? How do these explanations reflect the different points of view of the passages? Use details from both passages to support your answer. **Sample answer:** Both passages have different explanations about why the Berlin Wall was taken down. "The Berlin Wall" states that "Communism was failing across Europe" and that the East German government was facing "increasing opposition." However, the passage states that the Berlin Wall itself was taken down because of a mistake. In 1989, a German official "mistakenly" said that people could pass through the wall. When thousands of people arrived, the "guards were unprepared and eventually opened the gates." This explanation shows that the author views the passage as a general overview of history and does not want to explore the reasons for events too deeply. On the other hand, "Tear Down This Wall!" explains that the Berlin Wall was taken down in part because of the words and actions of President Reagan. The passage explains Reagan's efforts to improve relations with the Soviet Union and, most importantly, describes his 1987 speech at the wall in which he told Gorbachev to "open this gate" and "tear down this wall." According to the passage, this speech was "a turning point" in the Cold War and helped move Germany closer to freedom. This explanation reflects the author's view of Reagan as an important figure who was able to help change the course of events in history.	**RI.5.1, RI.5.6**